Baby Play
for Every Day

365 activities
for the
first year

Baby Play
for Every Day

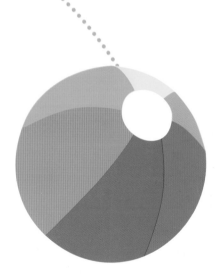

365 activities for the first year

DK

LONDON NEW YORK MUNICH
MELBOURNE DELHI

Author Susannah Steel
Expert Consultant Dr. Claire Halsey
Design by Emma and Tom Forge

US Editor Jane Perlmutter-MacPherson
US Consultant Dr. Aviva Schein
US Senior Editor Shannon Beatty

Senior Editor Victoria Heyworth-Dunne
Design Assistant Laura Buscemi
Senior Producer, Pre-Production Tony Phipps
Senior Producer Jen Scothern
Creative Technical Support Sonia Charbonnier
Managing Art Editor Christine Keilty
Creative Publishing Manager Anna Davidson
Art Director Jane Bull
Publisher Peggy Vance

First American edition, 2015

First published in the United States by DK Publishing,
345 Hudson Street, New York,
New York 10014

16 17 18   10 9 8 7 6 5 4 3 2
007 – 620877 – Jan/2015

Published in Great Britain by Dorling Kindersley Limited.

A catalog record for this book is available from the Library
of Congress.

ISBN 978–1–4654–2969–8

DK books are available at special discounts when purchased
in bulk for sales promotions, premiums, fund-raising, or
educational use. For details, contact: DK Publishing Special
Markets, 345 Hudson Street, 4th Floor, New York, New York
10014 or SpecialSales@dk.com.

Printed and bound in China

All images © Dorling Kindersley Limited
For further information see: www.dkimages.com

Discover more at **www.dk.com**

Disclaimer
The publisher and author disclaim any responsibility
for injuries, accidents, or damages resulting directly or
indirectly from the games and activities described and
illustrated in this book. Appropriate and reasonable
supervision of children at all times based on the age
and capability of the child is recommended.

Contents

Foreword

It is my pleasure to introduce you to this book of baby play. Having worked with children and families for nearly 30 years, and as a mother myself, I know how invaluable this accessible resource of practical play ideas will be to help you keep your baby entertained and learning through this wonderful first year. Play can be as simple or complex as suits you and your baby, and the themes and ideas in this book will support you whatever your preference.

I have loved every minute of working on the ideas you'll find in the coming pages. I've drawn on my experience of keeping my own three boys busy and learning, and on my knowledge and experience in child development, which informs each idea and tip.

Within each chapter you'll find activities that benefit your baby in the realms of speech and language, fine and gross motor skills, building relationships, and encouraging thinking and problem solving. It's great to know that play promotes development, but as you try out the ideas in this book, bear in mind that enjoyment, fun, and closeness are key to successful playtime.

We've focused mainly on activities that are simple to create or set up and rely on many everyday items. We also recognize that a stimulating home environment is a perfect place in which your baby can play, as is your own yard or nearest green space. Whether you have one baby, twins, or more, you'll find play ideas here to suit the situation with the minimum set-up time and maximum play value—something that's important when you are juggling the tasks of being a parent.

My favorite idea, one developed when my children were young and we had limited outdoor play space, is the suitcase sandbox (page 204). It was such a nice surprise for my children when we opened up the suitcase to reveal a sandbox with a few toys scattered on top. We got plenty of use from that suitcase—with some mess, of course—and I have lasting memories of the fun we had.

Of course, being a parent isn't all fun and games. No parent is immune to feeling bored sometimes, perhaps exhausted as sleepless nights or an unsettled baby take their toll, or simply at a loss about how to keep an eager baby entertained. That's why, in the pages to come, you'll find an array of fresh ideas, or a twist on something you may have already tried. Our goal is to lift the pressure on you to think up a completely new activity every time. Dip into these pages and let these suggestions do some of the work for you. I hope you find this book inspiring and valuable, and that you and your baby enjoy this precious year together.

How to use this book

The activities in this book are intended to give you ideas for fun and creative things to do with your baby. A happy baby flourishes with a happy parent, however, so we've also included a few ideas to make your life as a parent easier and more enjoyable.

You can either work through each chapter as your baby hits the appropriate month, or dip in and out of the book, picking activities according to you and your baby's mood and skill development. If you decide to dip in and out, make sure you look for ideas that suit your baby's particular developmental stage.

All babies develop at different rates, so you must be guided by what your baby enjoys. If her skills aren't developed enough for a particular activity, you should wait until she reaches the appropriate developmental stage. Stay with your baby throughout every activity, supervise her closely, and be especially vigilant around water.

Whatever activities you decide on each day, it is your active involvement in her play, enjoyment of your time together, and the warmth of your relationship that makes playtime special to your baby.

Your baby's amazing journey

Play and playfulness form the basis of your baby's development during the first months of her life. Why is play so important? Your baby has arrived primed to learn. Her brain is developing at the fastest rate she'll ever experience and it's through play that she'll soak up most of the information she needs to make sense of her world. When you play with your baby you offer her opportunities to explore, experiment, and experience. As you play together, and perhaps without consciously realizing it, you're fueling her senses and providing essential stimulation for her brain development.

Over the coming year, as your play activities together change and evolve, you'll be rewarded by advances in your baby's speech and language, her knowledge of the world around her, and her awareness of her body and how to control it. You'll also notice her relationships with others strengthen and her bond with you deepening.

This chart shows some of the major developmental milestones your baby will reach by 18 months. It's useful to remember, though, that babies naturally develop at different rates and your baby may reach her milestones a little earlier or later than other babies.

The developmental milestones listed here are approximate, but if your baby's progress is starting to concern you, seek advice from your pediatrician. In most cases you'll be reassured that she's doing fine or, for a few infants, early difficulties may be picked up and practical help offered.

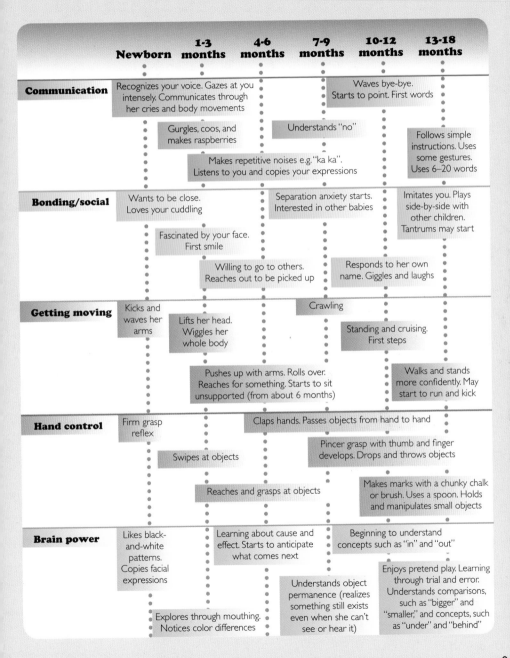

	Newborn	1-3 months	4-6 months	7-9 months	10-12 months	13-18 months
Communication	Recognizes your voice. Gazes at you intensely. Communicates through her cries and body movements	Gurgles, coos, and makes raspberries	Makes repetitive noises e.g. "ka ka". Listens to you and copies your expressions	Understands "no"	Waves bye-bye. Starts to point. First words	Follows simple instructions. Uses some gestures. Uses 6–20 words
Bonding/social	Wants to be close. Loves your cuddling	Fascinated by your face. First smile	Willing to go to others. Reaches out to be picked up	Separation anxiety starts. Interested in other babies	Responds to her own name. Giggles and laughs	Imitates you. Plays side-by-side with other children. Tantrums may start
Getting moving	Kicks and waves her arms	Lifts her head. Wiggles her whole body	Pushes up with arms. Rolls over. Reaches for something. Starts to sit unsupported (from about 6 months)	Crawling	Standing and cruising. First steps	Walks and stands more confidently. May start to run and kick
Hand control	Firm grasp reflex	Swipes at objects	Reaches and grasps at objects	Claps hands. Passes objects from hand to hand	Pincer grasp with thumb and finger develops. Drops and throws objects	Makes marks with a chunky chalk or brush. Uses a spoon. Holds and manipulates small objects
Brain power	Likes black-and-white patterns. Copies facial expressions	Explores through mouthing. Notices color differences	Learning about cause and effect. Starts to anticipate what comes next	Understands object permanence (realizes something still exists even when she can't see or hear it)	Beginning to understand concepts such as "in" and "out"	Enjoys pretend play. Learning through trial and error. Understands comparisons, such as "bigger" and "smaller," and concepts, such as "under" and "behind"

Your baby at...
0-1 months

As a small newborn coming to terms with life, your baby is completely focused on *connecting* with you. He quickly **recognizes** your voice, smell, and face, and may try to *mirror* your facial expressions.

He also needs your **love** and **reassurance** to feel secure. *Cuddling* and *talking* to him will encourage him to thrive: he'll love being *close* to you and enjoy the **soothing tones** of your voice.

by this age
your baby is probably able to:

🌸 Make eye contact with you

🌸 Recognize your face and bold,
contrasting patterns up close

🌸 Copy your facial movements

🌸 Know your smell

🌸 Recognize the sound of your voice

🌸 Be sensitive to touch

🌸 Use his instinctive reflexes
of turning his head, rooting, and
grasping with his hands (palmar reflex)

Some babies may even be able to:

🌸 Discern sweet and sour tastes

🌸 Use different cries to attract your attention

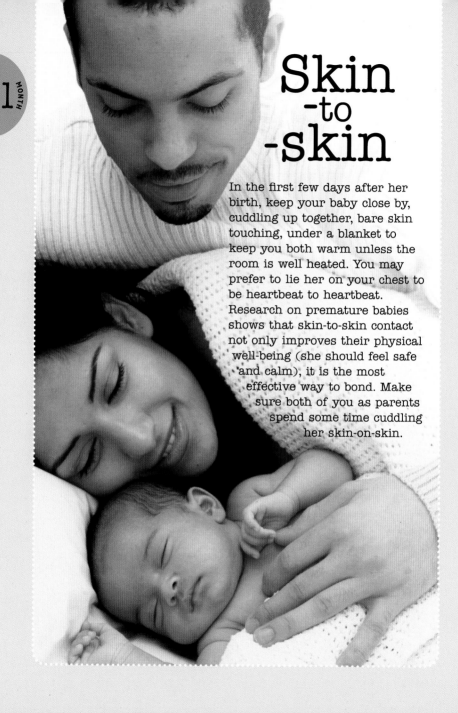

Skin -to -skin

In the first few days after her birth, keep your baby close by, cuddling up together, bare skin touching, under a blanket to keep you both warm unless the room is well heated. You may prefer to lie her on your chest to be heartbeat to heartbeat. Research on premature babies shows that skin-to-skin contact not only improves their physical well-being (she should feel safe and calm), it is the most effective way to bond. Make sure both of you as parents spend some time cuddling her skin-on-skin.

Test her grasp reflex

Your newborn's reflexes are already developed: she'll try to grip anything you place in the palm of her hand. Let her wrap her hand around your finger, take a photograph, and frame it or stick it in an album or journal for posterity.

Memory box

Start a box of mementos for your baby. Include your prenatal scans, her hospital bracelet—perhaps even the soap you used in hospital as an olfactory reminder. Add more items—a first tooth, an invitation to her Christening or naming ceremony, a lock of hair, baby booties, a shell from her first visit to beach, a first toy—anything that tells her personal story.

Birth recovery
for your baby

Recovering from the birth and dealing with a new world is a big adjustment for your baby—and for you as new parents. Make rest and relaxation a priority in these first weeks. Try a peaceful yoga pose or two (good if you have had a cesarian section) to recoup energy levels, disperse any tensions, and feel calm together. Repeat them as often as you like through the day.

Hugging stretch

Lie on your back on a rug or soft surface with a pillow or cushion under your head and neck so you feel supported and comfortable. Lay your baby face down on your chest with his head gently resting to one side. Bend your knees and keep your feet flat on the floor to protect your back. Gently fold your arms over your baby and hold him. Breathe deeply and as you exhale slowly, bring your shoulders down and press the base of your spine against the floor to ease any tension in your back. Repeat four times, then relax.

Relaxed baby

Lie in the same position (on your back, with knees bent, feet flat on the floor, and head supported), with your baby lying on his tummy on your chest so you are heartbeat-to-heartbeat. Check that you are both as comfortable as possible. Hold him gently, close your eyes, and breathe slowly in and out. Try not to move too much and rest deeply for as long you both enjoy it.

First
sensations

Gently stroke your baby's arms, hands, and feet in a soothing motion while she is nursing and she'll love the gentle touch of your fingers on her skin. Also try stroking a soft cotton ball on the backs of her hands and fingertips to give her a different sensation.

Spend time alone with your baby

As a parent, you need to spend some one-on-one time with your baby to establish a strong bond, understand her language, and feel involved in her care. There's no need to do anything complicated—spending time just looking at her, making eye contact, and talking to her is the best way for you to get to know each other.

Start
talking

Cooing and speaking "parentese" to your baby from birth is vital for her speech development. Research shows that the long, clear sounds parents speak to their newborn is a key part of the language process. So don't feel embarassed about using singsong speech and exaggerated facial expressions to produce long vowels and clear changes in tone as you speak to her.

Begin your
baby journal

You will notice something different about your baby each day, so write it down in a journal and stick in photos you love. Though it may seem very early to start a journal, adding notes and photos week by week—or month by month—quickly helps to build her history. You won't forget what she is like now if you have prompts to jog your memory later on, and you will be able to treasure her first year. If you have twins, take photos of them together and separately; they'll want to see photos of their sibling, but also follow their own story.

Sing a lullaby

Make eye contact with your baby and sing him a lullaby or song as you put him down to sleep. Have a small number of favorites ready so he quickly gets used to the rhythm and words of the lullaby and the soothing tone of your voice. You could try "Hush, Little Baby," "Rock-a-Bye Baby," "Baa, Baa, Black Sheep," and "Swing Low, Sweet Chariot," or simple favorites such as "Twinkle Twinkle Little Star."

Take a neighborhood walk

Pop your baby into a baby carrier, or sling, facing you (or in his stroller), and take him for a short walk through your neighborhood, talking to him all the while and telling him about any local landmarks. He'll love the sound of your voice and the motion should soothe him.

Eat well

To give you enough energy to care for your baby, eat healthy, nutrient-dense snacks regularly. If you are breast-feeding, your baby will directly benefit from this type of food. Try these instant snacks (which can all be eaten with one hand) to keep your glucose levels, and therefore your mood, stable:

- Hummus with pitas and raw vegetables such as carrot sticks, broccoli florets, and sliced red pepper
- Whole-grain tortilla wrap filled with sliced chicken or turkey and avocado
- Bagel with salmon and cream cheese
- Whole-grain toast with a nut butter spread
- Banana and some raw, unsalted nuts
- Apple and a couple of slices of cheese

Try these...

Stay hydrated

Drink plenty of liquids to maintain the energy levels you need to take care of your baby. Water is the best way to hydrate, and milk, juice, and decaffeinated and herbal teas are fine in moderation. If you are breast-feeding, avoid caffeine, since it can get into your baby's system, and avoid licorice tea if you have high blood pressure.

Mirror your baby's expression

Hold your baby, look into her eyes, and copy her gaze—her wide eyes, perhaps, or her blinking. She may copy you back, since she's already trying to read your face.

Baby in space

Take your baby for a tour around the house. As you walk, support her neck and head and very gently dip and raise her—her brain and body are already receptive to learning how her body moves in different directions.

Share the hugs

Hugging your baby is one of the most important things you can do as a parent. However, she needs cuddling from everyone in your immediate family so that she gets to know their feel and smell too. Remember, too, that you also need physical affection and care from loved ones.

Light
and shade

Lay your baby on her back near a window, maybe with a tree directly outside, where she can look up and gaze at the contrasts in light and shade. In these first weeks she can already determine patterns and strong contrasts in tone.

Stick your tongues out

Catch your baby's attention and stick your tongue out every 20 seconds or so. Although it may take a minute or two, she should respond by sticking her tongue out at you!

Ask questions

Jot down any questions or concerns about your baby that come to mind so you have them on hand and don't forget about them while your pediatrician is with you.

Tracking game

During her first month, your baby's eyesight improves from only seeing things close-up to being able to focus about 8–15 in (20–35 cm) away—the right distance to be able to see your face when you hold and feed her. Stimulate her brain and sharpen her visual skills by getting her to follow your face with her eyes. Hold her in your arms, attract her attention by talking to her, slowly move your head from side to side, and see if she can track your head movements.

Help him discover
his hands

Hold your baby's hands in yours, or let him grip your fingers, and move them gently from side-to-side to soothing music. He'll watch his hands—and you—as he begins to discover this part of his body, even though he doesn't yet realize his hands are connected to his body.

Give your baby a
hand massage

Gently open up your baby's hands and massage his palms using a plant-based or edible oil such olive oil. (For the best oil to use, ask your pediatrician, but avoid oils likely to cause a reaction such as peanut, paraffin, sesame, and essential oils.)

Pacify
your baby

If your baby is crying and you don't know why, try this relaxing yoga pose and gently hum or sing over him.

It's also a good idea to sing to him every time you change his diaper or do a quick chore—he will love to listen to the sounds you make and won't mind if you are not a natural singer.

Calming pose

Lay your baby on his back on a soft surface such as a sheepskin or an extra-soft blanket or towel. Make sure he is warm and comfortable. Kneel down on all fours and bend over him so that your elbows and palms are resting on either side of him on the sheepskin and your face is close to his. Gently hum and sing over him to help pacify him. Try to lengthen your out-breaths as you sing to allow you to release any tension you may be holding, and enjoy the stretch through your spine if your back is feeling sore or stiff.

Make a "baby napping" sign

If the doorbell rings frequently and disturbs your sleeping baby, make a sign on a piece of cardboard in indelible ink saying "Baby napping—please visit another time," and stick it on the front door while she sleeps.

If you have a busy family home, make a similar sign to hang on the bedroom door to let the rest of the family know when she is sleeping or feeding.

Draw a simple face

Your baby likes looking at faces more than anything else. Draw a simple face in thick black felt-tip on a piece of white card stock and hold it about 12 in (30 cm) from her face. She'll be fascinated by the image.

24

Leopard
in a tree

Try laying your baby on her front along your forearm with your hand supporting her head (or rest her head on your forearm by your elbow and support her body with both hands). If carrying her like a "leopard in a tree" comes naturally to you and she feels secure, try swaying her gently from side to side.

Bird's-eye view

If you prefer to try holding your baby another way, put her over your shoulder. Keep one hand under her bottom to carry her weight and use your other hand to support her head next to yours. Then walk her around and let her see the world from over your shoulder.

Show your baby this page

Looking at these bold contrasting patterns will help him practice focusing his eyes and develop his spacial awareness.

Give her time to develop her gaze

As you feed your baby or hold her in your arms, give her plenty of time to look up and study your face. Her focus is improving all the time, so you may find her gazing up at your hairline if you have dark hair, and her eyes may move around your face for some time.

Learn her language

Spend today learning what your baby is trying to tell you, and as you respond to her signals she'll learn that it's important to communicate. You'll know if she's content, but the pitch of her cry may mean she's hungry or wants to be held close, and she may rub her eyes if she's tired. If she frowns, yawns, or turns her head, she's had enough play.

Check the diaper bag

You may be more confident about taking your baby out and about now. To help you get out of the house more quickly, look through your diaper bag after each trip out and replenish the wipes, diapers, and burp cloths right away. If you get into the habit of doing this, the bag will be ready to use at a moment's notice, and is one less thing to deal with before you leave.

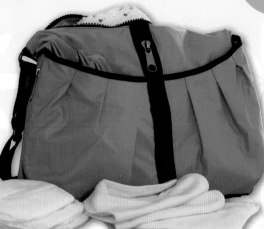

Let your baby get moving

Lay your baby on her back on a soft rug on the floor in a warm room with just her diaper, and perhaps a onesie, on so she can learn how to move her body. She'll try to kick her legs, wave her arms, and perhaps punch the air. Giving her opportunities to move freely every day is great practice for her muscles and coordination skills.

29

Your baby at...
1-2 months

Now he's a few weeks old, your baby is learning about **muscle control**: he may be able to *lift* and *move* his **head** a little, and make **slightly smoother movements**. He'll use his **voice** and **body language** to show he's *excited* when he senses you are around, and he may respond with *cooing noises* when you talk to him. His **improving eyesight** means he is beginning to *track* objects in front of his face. He is also **becoming aware** of other important people in his life.

by this age
your baby is probably able to:

🌸 Move his head from side to side

🌸 Coo in response to you

🌸 Use the movements of his body to communicate with you

🌸 See things a little further away

🌸 Start developing bonds with other family members or familiar people

🌸 Give his first smile

🌸 Open and close his mouth in imitation of you when you talk to him

Some babies may even be able to:
🌸 Look up briefly during tummy time

Stop!

Stop
and watch

Take a few moments to stop whatever
you are doing and focus fully on your baby.
Watch how her control over her movements is
improving, the way her expression is becoming
more alert, and marvel at how quickly she recognizes you.
Try to make this a daily habit, since there is so much to enjoy
that is easily missed in the busy whirl of early parenthood.

Meet new friends

Young babies are intrigued by other children. If your baby has siblings or cousins, let them stroke her while she's in your arms. They may even enjoy a special role as your helper by passing you diaper wipes or a clean diaper, and talking to their baby sister while you change her. Or invite friends and their toddlers or young children over for some bonding time; your baby will be entertained by any child if they are playing nearby.

Visual stimulation

Your baby's eyesight is improving fast, and she can now see objects a little farther away, distinguish the colors red, green, and yellow, and focus on distinctive shapes. Choose a baby gym with brightly colored toys and let her enjoy lying beneath the dangling objects to try to focus on them.

Baby
aerobics

Help your baby strengthen his legs, arms, and abdominal muscles with some baby aerobics. Don't be discouraged if he doesn't seem enthusiastic at first; try again later and he may respond to your gentle touch and encouraging voice and smile by relaxing his limbs. Make sure the room is warm and try doing these gentle, minimal exercises to the rhythm of a song or nursery rhyme, such as "Baa, Baa, Black Sheep," to hold his attention and keep his gaze on you.

Lift and lower his limbs

Lay him on his back on a soft surface on the floor and kneel down in front of him. Hold his hands in yours and very gently lift and lower his hands a few times. Cup a foot in each hand—or both feet in your hands—and lift and lower his feet in the same way.

Still holding his feet, lift them off the floor a little. Gently move his feet slightly away from each other, bring them back together, and lower them to the floor. Repeat a few more times.

Circle his
hands and feet

Lift his hands up slightly and very gently move his arms in small circles. Then circle his feet in the same way.

Keep singing or repeating a nursery rhyme—or talk to him softly if he responds better.

Pedal his legs
and rock his knees

Lift his feet up so his legs are in the air. Gently rotate his legs alternately in a bicycling motion for a short time. Finish by gently bringing his knees up toward his chest a few times so his bottom just lifts off the floor. These movements are especially good if he suffers from colic or needs to burp or get rid of any gas.

Turn cooing into a game

Hold or rest your baby in her bouncy chair in front of you so you are looking straight into each other's eyes. Make a clear cooing sound, exaggerating your facial expression as you do. If she responds with a similar sound, repeat it back to her. Make more sounds back and forth for as long as she remains interested. Playing with clear vocal sounds like this helps her to distinguish speech from other noises.

Bond more deeply

So much has happened in your baby's short life that her birth may seem like it was ages ago. Look at your prenatal scans and photos of her as a newborn to revisit the feelings of awe she inspired. Or you may want to recall the moment when you saw she was safe, or a happy memory soon after she was born. In additon to being a positive experience (and helping you work through any mixed feelings you may have about the birth itself), this process releases the hormone oxytocin—known to stimulate feelings of attachment—in your brain to actively deepen your bond with her.

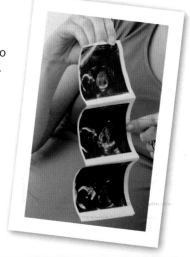

Kisses to learn

Whenever you dress your baby or change her diaper, say, "I love your tummy," and kiss her tummy. Repeat several times, then kiss her hands, feet, forehead, ears, cheeks, and nose in the same way as you talk to her. Combining touch and speech like this helps her both listen to language and enjoy affection.

Read aloud

If you want to read a newspaper, the sports pages, or a magazine while your baby is awake and contented, read aloud. It doesn't matter what you read to her when she is this tiny, she just wants to hear your familiar voice and the long, clear sounds you make.

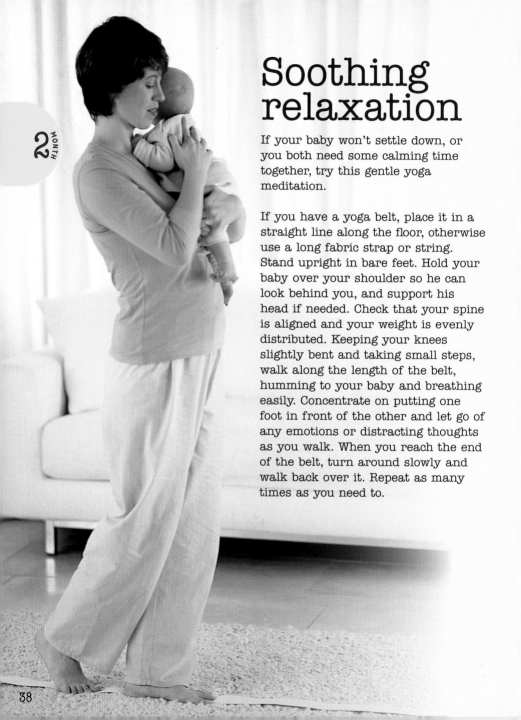

Soothing relaxation

If your baby won't settle down, or you both need some calming time together, try this gentle yoga meditation.

If you have a yoga belt, place it in a straight line along the floor, otherwise use a long fabric strap or string. Stand upright in bare feet. Hold your baby over your shoulder so he can look behind you, and support his head if needed. Check that your spine is aligned and your weight is evenly distributed. Keeping your knees slightly bent and taking small steps, walk along the length of the belt, humming to your baby and breathing easily. Concentrate on putting one foot in front of the other and let go of any emotions or distracting thoughts as you walk. When you reach the end of the belt, turn around slowly and walk back over it. Repeat as many times as you need to.

Record your baby

Take short bursts of footage of your baby's everyday activities—lying on his back kicking his legs in the air, for example, or taking a bath in his baby bath. You will treasure these seemingly mundane moments in years to come.

Try these...

Sound idea

Your baby's hearing is well developed at birth, and by six weeks or so she may be trying to find out where you are if she can hear your voice but can't see you. Try this game to help her coordinate her hearing and eyesight: put her in her baby chair or bouncy seat on the floor and talk to her from different points in the room. See if she turns her head to try to locate where you are.

Trade top tips

Get together with friends, or join a parenting group if your friends haven't yet had babies (see Resources), to share ideas about taking care of a baby; you'll have the satisfaction of helping others, and learn new tips.

Dance to a rhythm

Play some relaxing music that you enjoy moving to. Either sit with your baby supported in your lap and swing together, or stand up with her in your arms and gently move around, supporting her neck if needed.

Baby face

Buy some bright felt, cut out a large circle, and make a simple face by cutting holes for a nose, mouth, and eyes—or use a piece of boldly patterned material instead. Attach the material to the inside of your baby's carriage hood for her to look up at when you are out walking.

Scarf play

If you are wearing a scarf, take it off with a flourish and let the tassled end dangle near your baby. Try tickling her hand with the tassles to catch her attention, then hold the scarf steady and see if she reaches out to feel it and tries to swipe at it.

Join a local library

Reading books to your young baby is a wonderful way of interacting and bonding with her. By reading out loud and talking about the pictures in a book, you are also familiarizing her with sounds and language from a very early age. If you aren't already a member, join your local library and choose a small selection of board books with big, bold pictures without much background detail.

Introduce the family

Aunts, uncles, and cousins can all start to form part of your baby's wider family social circle now. Introduce them one at a time and give your baby the chance to look at their face and make eye contact as she begins to get to know them.

Add to your journal

Try to fill in your baby's journal whenever you get the chance so you don't forget the precious memories of these early months: her eyes and hair color may be changing; her first real smile may appear; and she may be making new sounds.

First smiles

Watch for your baby's first real smile this month. If you keep smiling at his face whenever you look at him, he will directly respond at some point by using his whole face, including his eyes, to smile back at you. If you reward his smile by smiling back enthusiastically, he's much more likely to do it again. Smiling is one of his earliest social exchanges; enjoy these first smiles as he learns how to show you he's happy and watches for your reaction.

Take a bath
with your baby

Being snuggled against his parent's chest at bath time can make all the difference if your baby doesn't enjoy his own baby bath very much. Make sure the water is the right temperature for him before you get in together, and make lots of soothing noises as you bathe him and gently splash water over his tummy.

Be a
kangaroo

If you have a baby who doesn't settle down unless someone is cuddling him, strap him into a baby carrier, or sling, and continue with any activities you have to get done. Don't be afraid to gently bounce, cuddle, hold, and sway him as you move around, and keep talking softly to him if he is awake.

Calm baby

If your baby is showing signs that she's overstimulated, bored, or tired and in need of being held, turn off any background noise like the TV or radio—or take her to a quieter room—so she can only hear the sound of your voice. Hold her and talk to her in a low voice, or sing very gently. Hearing your voice and being so close to you will help reduce her stress level and keep her alert. If she relaxes completely, she may lie peacefully in your arms and look intently into your eyes, showing you that she is feeling calm and content.

Tracking toys

Gently move a toy across your baby's line of vision, softly rustling, rattling, or squeaking it as you go, and see if she can track the toy with her eyes. If her eyes follow the object, dangle a few different objects in front of her for her to try to swipe at or kick as she learns how to extend her limbs and use her hands. Use everyday objects, such as a bright ball of yarn, ribbon, or even a sparkly present decoration bow, as well as baby toys.

Play
The Itsy Bitsy Spider

Repeat this simple rhyme as you walk your fingers up and down each of your baby's arms in turn and end with a gentle tickle and big smile. She will love to watch your face, soon grow accustomed to the repetitive sounds, and begin to express her delight at the game:

"The itsy bitsy spider
Climbed up the water spout.
Down came the rain,
And washed the spider out.
Out came the sun,
And dried up all the rain,
So the itsy bitsy spider
Climbed up the spout again!"

Where are you?

Lie on your back on the bed or floor and lay your baby on her front on your chest with your hands around her middle. Hold your head up so you can see your baby. Call her name and raise her body up slightly to encourage her to lift her head a little to see you. Repeat a couple more times, praising her if she looks at you. Raising her head is the first movement she learns to control, and is necessary for the next stage of her motor development.

Mirror faces

Lay your baby on his back on a soft blanket or rug and lie down on your back next to him so your heads are touching and you are both looking up. Hold up a large hand mirror so you can both look up into it. Make eye contact with him in the mirror, calling his name to catch his attention if necessary. Smile brightly at him in the mirror and watch his expression change. If he smiles back, give him lots of praise.

Try making other exaggerated facial expressions to see how he reacts—raise your eyebrows, or widen your eyes, for example. From birth, your baby loves looking at your face; this game helps him learn a different way of looking at you, and reinforces his recognition of facial features.

47

Face to face

Whether you use a baby carrier or sling, or convertable carriage-stroller, let your baby see your face often. Lift her up in her carrier, supporting her head if needed, so she can see your face, watch your expression, the movement of your mouth as you speak, and hear you easily, which is important for her own speech and language development. If your carriage is forward-facing, turn it around so she faces you every time you stop or park the carriage.

Instant entertainment

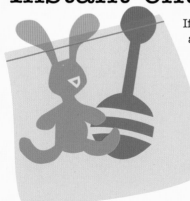

If you are going out and about for a while today, put a sealed ziplock bag of one or two toys—maybe a rattle, small soft toy, or squeezy toy—in your diaper bag. She's already attracted to movement and sounds, so use these toys to distract, occupy, or soothe her as needed.

Try some "on" time

Your baby is still fascinated by looking at people's faces. Let her enjoy having some "on" time with someone else while you have some time "off." Arrange for a partner, grandparent, or close friend to babysit for an hour while you stay close by and enjoy some hands-free time catching up on email or household management, or relax.

Repeat a simple story

Whether you make up your own simple story or read a story from a baby book, repeat it several times over so your baby can hear the same sounds over again. She will love the repetitious sounds you make, and may even try to imitate your speech by opening and closing her mouth as you talk.

Your baby at...
2-3 months

Your baby may be noticing his *hands* around now, learning that he can *open* and *close* them and **play with his fingers**. He may also be **experimenting** with making different *sounds* as he tries to respond to your chats with him. He may even **surprise you** with his **first *giggles*** and **gurgles.** As his **muscle control** in his **neck** improves, he will now be *turning* his **head** from **side to side** and *lifting* his head briefly during **tummy time.**

by this age
your baby is probably able to:

* Smile back at you
* Move his arms and legs more confidently
* Stretch out to try to grasp toys
* Clasp an object placed in his hand
* Discern primary and bright colours
* Use a range of facial expressions
* Giggle

Some babies may even be able to:

* Lift their head up to a 90-degree angle when lying on their stomachs during tummy time
* Reach out to grab something

51

Unwind
outside

On a warm, dry day, let your baby sleep
outside in her carriage in the shade, in the
yard or in a local park, while you relax beside
her. Take a folding chair with you if there
isn't an outside seat or bench, and let
the sounds of the natural world help
you unwind a little. Or take a picnic
blanket and lie together under a leafy
tree. Look up through the leaves
at the sky and describe what
you can see to her.

Indoor sledding

Place a large piece of cardboard on a carpet or rug (checking first that there are no staples of other sharp objects in the cardboard). Lay your baby face down on the cardboard with her arms out in front of her or to her sides and move the cardboard gently side to side to give the sensation of sliding. She may lift her head for a few seconds if her neck muscles are getting stronger to see what is going on!

White noise

If your baby is overstimulated and finding it hard to go down for a nap, turn on the vacuum cleaner or washing machine and let the white noise from the machine help to lull her to sleep.

Play with finger puppets

For the first of many animated (and, for now, one-sided) conversations, make finger puppets from colorful felt to entertain your baby. He will adore watching these puppets wiggling on your fingers as you talk about each animal, make relevant noises, and conjure up simple stories about them. Always keep the puppets well out of his reach.

1 Draw a head template, plus any key animal features, on tracing paper. Cut them out, pin them onto felt, and cut around them using sharp scissors.

2 Cut out two head pieces for each puppet. Sew the felt features—snout, nostrils, teeth, stripes, and so on, plus eyes, onto the front of each puppet with a needle and thread.

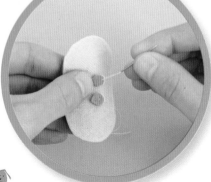

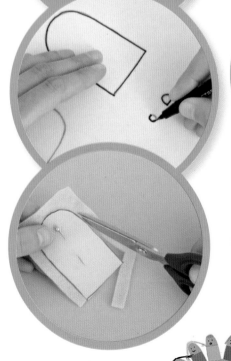

3

Align the two head pieces for each animal and sew them together, leaving the shortest edge open to insert your finger. Sew on any final touches such as ears and a mane.

MONTH **3**

Customize her
baby gym

As your baby starts to kick and swipe more confidently, her baby gym will be getting plenty of use. Customize the gym by switching the toys around, and hang some new objects from it. Choose age-appropriate toys with baby velcro straps if needed, attach them on securely, and let some dangle down so she can reach them occasionally with her hands while she's lying on her back.

Floating scarf

Fling a floaty scarf into the air and let it fall around your baby. Tell her what is happening and encourage her to look up as the scarf floats down. Repeat a few times and watch her face to see if she's enjoying the sensation. Try also using a feather boa or some feathers from an art-supply store to create the same effect.

Butterfly kisses

Give your baby butterfly kisses on her cheeks when you have some calm cuddling time together. Bring your eyes up close to her cheek and flutter your lashes so they delicately stroke her skin. She will love the closeness of being with you, and be curious about the tickling sensations on her skin.

Up and away

Sit on the floor, knees bent, with your baby resting on her tummy against your shins. Hold her hands in yours, exhale, and use your abdominals to roll gently backward to lie on your back on the floor. Keep your knees bent the whole time. As you roll back, your knees will lift in the air, taking your baby with you so she rises up, still resting against your shins. Make lots of encouraging noises to keep her attention. If your abdominals are strong enough, roll back up after a short while, otherwise lift her off your shins and give her a hug.

Hang a mobile

Buy or make a mobile and hang from the ceiling in your baby's
nursery or sleeping area for him to look up at.

To make a homemade mobile, cut shapes—perhaps teddy bears,
elephants, cats, balloons, clowns, and boats (traced from books
if you want to use a template)—from brightly colored felt. Sew
on any features with a needle and thread, and attach a string
to the top of each shape. Open out a stripy toy umbrella and turn
it upside down. Attach the loose end of each length of string to
an umbrella spoke. Hang the umbrella mobile very securely
from the ceiling, and make sure that your baby can't reach
the umbrella or felt shapes from his crib.

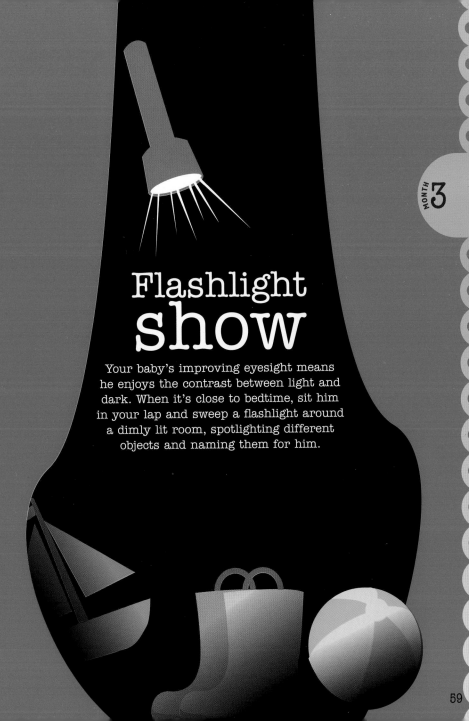

Flashlight
show

Your baby's improving eyesight means
he enjoys the contrast between light and
dark. When it's close to bedtime, sit him
in your lap and sweep a flashlight around
a dimly lit room, spotlighting different
objects and naming them for him.

Try these...

Join a local parent and baby group

When you join a local parent and baby group, your baby will have a greater choice of different toys and new faces to enjoy. Talk to your pediatrician, look online, or check the information board at your library or community center to find a good local group. Try different groups to find one that's right for you both, since they can vary a lot.

First giggles

Your baby is motivated to copy you, so try to make her giggle. Poke out your tongue, smile, raise your eyebrows, and laugh to show her you are having fun. She may respond with her first giggle.

Color vision

Your baby is starting to tell the difference between more subtle shades—orange and red, for example. Keep offering her toys of different colors to catch her attention and entertain her.

Touching sensation

As she gains more control of her arms, hands, and fingers, your baby wants to touch everything, including you. Move closer if she wants to touch your face, and smile at her to encourage her. Be careful though—she hasn't yet learned how to let go!

Changing world

Spend some quiet time with your baby watching the world go by together, and enjoy these peaceful moments. Whether you're outside or indoors looking through a window, sit her on your lap so she can look out. Talk softly to her, describing what you see and pointing to objects and people close by.

Book swap

Now that her focus is sharpening, swap your baby's first books for some new board books with pictures that contain slightly more detail and bold, contrasting colors.

Happy talk

Your baby may be making her first recognizable sounds as she experiments with her own voice. Keep talking to her and if she responds with some "eh" and "oh" vowel sounds, repeat them back to her so she is encouraged to say more.

Entertain your baby

Dance for, or with, your baby to music you enjoy. Use exaggerated hand movements, like jazz hands, and big facial expressions to be as comical as possible. She will love watching you having fun and laughing. If there are two of you, one of you may want to carry her in your arms and rock her to the music while the other dances as energetically as they want.

Noisy toys

Your baby is at the earliest stage of learning about cause and effect. Give her a noisy toy such as a rattle to hold and shake. She'll soon register that her action results in a reaction.

quack

Roly poly play

To give your baby a new sensation, gently roll him over on a blanket, bed, or on some soft grass in the yard. He'll soon be rolling himself over once he gains enough strength.

Touch
and feel

Everything your baby touches builds his knowledge, so let him discover some new tactile objects. Brush a wool or furry toy across his bare tummy, for example, and describe what it feels like. As he feels it, he may want to reach for it to explore it further. Try other objects such as a soft, squashy toy, leather glove, or baby sensory ball.

Make simple
hand- and footprints

Now that your baby's hands have unfurled and are no longer in a natural fist, make prints of his hands and feet to stick in his baby journal. Use watercolor paper and water-based, child-friendly, nontoxic paint. If you have a special pottery painting store nearby, you may want to put his prints on mugs or plates as gifts for loved ones. Alternatively, buy a small prestretched canvas from an art store and make prints straight onto the canvas to hang on the wall.

First
instrument

shake!

3 MONTH

Fill a small plastic water bottle a quarter of the way up with some dried lentils. Replace the lid firmly. Put your baby's hands in yours and shake it together just a little to make a noise. Then sing one of her favorite nursery songs and shake the bottle yourself in time to the beat.

red sock

Sock play

Put a brightly colored sock on your baby's foot. Gently move her foot so she can see the sock, and tell her what color it is. She may try to grab the sock, and will be surprised if it pops off her foot.

Hand control

Your baby is fascinated by what she can do with her hands now: as her newborn grasping reflex fades, she can choose what she wants to grip onto. Hand her a baby book or toys with different textures to explore, or lower a toy on her baby gym so she can grab it.

Bond with Bach

Play some classical music and hold your baby as you move to the music. Turn the music down occasionally if you want to whisper words of love to her, then turn the music back up and continue to cuddle her or stroke her head and back. Listening to music like this may also encourage her brain development for math and spatial reasoning.

Tummy time

When his neck muscles are strong enough for him to lift and turn his head a little, lay him on his front on a firm, comfortable surface. Position yourself in front of and slightly above him, talk gently to him and call his name, or play soothing music, and let him lie on his tummy for a few minutes. Gradually extend the tummy time as he gets stronger: get down on the floor next to him with a few toys to engage his attention and help him begin to move.

Tummy time is important to your baby's development, because it's a precursor to crawling, standing, and walking. If he's not happy lying on his front when you first put him on the floor, lay him on his tummy on your chest (as you lie on your back on the floor), and talk to him. After a few times like this, he may be happy to try tummy time for himself on the floor again.

New sounds

3 MONTH

Develop your baby's concentration skills by letting her hear the noises of different household objects—an alarm clock, an electric shaver, the timer on a microwave or oven, the hum of a dishwasher, and water flowing from a faucet, for example. Tell her where the noise comes from as you listen to it together.

tick tock

Tower of blocks

Your baby's hand movements are becoming more refined. Build a simple tower of bright fabric blocks, then bat them over with your hand. Rebuild the tower and encourage her to copy you by swiping at the tower with her hands.

Ready, action

As a natural mimic, your baby will happily try to copy you. Prop him up, hold his hands in yours, and gently move his arms to one of his favorite action songs as you sing to him. He will love the repetition if you sing the song and do the actions several times.

Musical "hide-and-seek"

Your baby is becoming more adept at locating where sounds come from. Sit her in your lap and hold a rattle out to her left side where she can't see it. Gently shake the rattle and wait to see if she turns her head to find out where the sound comes from. Repeat several times on each side.

Your baby at...

3-4 months

From three months, your baby is starting to **reveal** something of his *personality* in the way he *expresses* himself through his voice and body language: he may **squeal** and **giggle** at his reflection, for example, or **gaze intently** at it. He is growing **stronger** and more **alert** now, *swiping* at objects with his **hands** and *exploring* them with his **mouth**. He's also happy to be **out and about** more, as long as he is *close to you*.

by this age
your baby is probably able to:

🌸 Control his head movements

🌸 Explore objects with his mouth

🌸 Notice different shades of colour

🌸 Gurgle, squeal, and blow raspberries

🌸 Smile to connect with other people

🌸 "Stand" on your knee and push up with his legs as you support him

🌸 Wriggle his body in excitement or anticipation

🌸 Push up on his arms during tummy time (as his arm and neck control improves)

Some babies may even be able to:

🌸 Be aware of their body in space as you move them in different directions

Exercise outdoors

Take your baby to an outdoor instructor-led parents' exercise class, if one is available in a park near you. Typically, your baby enjoys the fresh air and scenery from her stroller or carriage while you exercise beside her. If there is an outdoor gym in your park you could work out there; try a stationary bike or cross trainer for some moderate, low-impact exercise, and make sure your baby can see you from her stroller. Or why not go for a walk or run with her. Whatever you choose, it would be a change of scene for both of you and should help you gradually get back into shape.

4 MONTH

Tactile rhyme

Since touch is one of the most powerful ways in which you can bond with your baby, try tactile rhymes such as this whenever you get the chance. Touch her fingers, toes, ears, nose, and mouth, and then scoop her up in a hug and kiss her.

✿

"Ten little fingers, ten little toes,
Two little ears and one little nose,
Two little eyes that shine so bright,
And one little mouth to kiss me goodnight!"

Up-down walking tour

Walk your baby round the house or garden, gently turning around, and dipping and raising her as you go. Her senses are now very receptive to lessons about how her body moves through space. Every move she makes also helps to develop her coordination and balance, and exercise her muscles. Say "Up" and "Down" as you lift and lower her while you walk..

Sleepy baby

Now is a good time to establish a regular bedtime routine for your baby if you haven't done so already. Good sleep is key for him to process the day's play and activities, and enjoy more play time tomorrow.

Sleep is stimulus-dependent, so a bedtime routine is all-important—it needs to involve the same activities in the right order at roughly the same time every evening. Introduce story time and snuggle time after bath time and an evening feeding, before you put your baby to sleep in his crib. Make it as special as possible with slightly dimmed lights and a favorite book in a relaxing corner, for example. While you can swap bedtime duties with your partner as often as you both want, always follow the same routine, such as bath, feeding, story time, snuggle, kiss, and bed.

Reminder pad

If sleepless nights and the busyness of life are leaving you feeling foggy, stick a magnetic notepad or wipe-clean board on the fridge or somewhere prominent to add reminders to yourself about anything important you need to do for your baby. Include notes such as repacking the diaper bag, scheduling doctor's appointments, or buying more wet wipes.

Break open the bubbles

Blowing bubbles will provide your baby with hours of fun in the months ahead, and now is a perfect moment to introduce her to her very first bubbles. Either lie her flat and blow bubbles above her head so she can gaze up at them, or blow some bubbles while she is in the bath and let them pop around her.

Join a local music and movement class

Now is a good time to follow up you and your baby's enjoyment of music by joining a local parent and baby group, where you'll get the chance to sing and play with others. The social and musical elements will encourage your baby to make sounds and move. There may be free groups or classes available, so look online or in local venues such as libraries and community centers. Music and musical beats help your baby to develop an understanding of the patterns within speech.

Bouncing baby

Hold your baby securely around her middle and sit her on top of a stability ball (sports stores should have inexpensive versions, or you can buy one online or use a toy ball hopper). Bounce her gently up and down. This simple game can help her start to learn about where her body is in space, and will strengthen her tummy muscles.

Sensory adventure

If you or a grandparent has an outdoor clothesline—or space to attach a horizontal length of twine between two trees in the yard—hang up some soft towels and sheets, hold your baby in your arms, and carry him gently through the laundry. Allow a sheet or two to drape gently over his head and then "pop" out on the other side to create an element of surprise. Let him feel the soft material on his skin as you move along the clothesline, and talk about what you are doing as you walk along.

Visit an aquarium

Take a trip to an aquarium, or visit a friend with a fish tank, to watch brightly colored fish. Now that your baby can concentrate for short periods of time, he will be entranced by the fluorescent creatures swimming in front of him. Point out the different fish and describe what you can see as he watches them move.

Try these...

Visual reassurance

Textured toys

If your baby is beginning to grab hold of objects, give her different textured toys—such as a soft, squishy toy, a cool, smooth plastic toy, and a toy with a bumpy surface—to explore with her fingers and her mouth.

Hang a large laminated photo of yourself or your partner from the headrest of the back seat so your baby can look at the image while you drive. She will feel reassured by seeing a familiar face, and can be soothed by your voice when you speak to her.

Have a family meal together

Introduce a family meal, perhaps on the weekend, to get into the habit of eating together. Family mealtimes are not only hugely important for communicating and connecting with each other, they help your baby learn about table manners and how to eat; she may also be extremely interested in what you put in your mouth. Let her join in by putting her on your lap or in her baby seat beside you while you eat.

Sit-ups

Put your baby on her back on the floor and sit down opposite her. Hold her hands in yours and count "One, two, three" as you gently pull her to a sitting position. You may need to support her head as you gently lower her back down.

Try on-site
day care

This month—while she still sleeps a lot and before separation anxiety sets in—is a good time for your baby to try some day care. Look for a gym that has day care on-site to babysit her while you work out, swim, or go to an exercise class.

Let go, grab hold

If your baby is holding a small toy in her hand, pass her another one; she'll automatically drop the first to take the one offered. This is the start of her learning how to open her hand and let go.

Tasty toes

Gently stroke your baby's toes, then lie her on her back and encourage her to try to touch and grab her feet and even bring them to her mouth. Clap and praise her if she can coordinate this difficult move.

Introduce
peekaboo

For a simple game of cause and effect, put a towel or scarf in front of your face and let your baby pull it away with your help. Express surprise and say "Peekaboo!" as the cloth falls away.

Try some new
sounds

Your baby may be making cooing sounds now. Make cooing noises or click your tongue several times and encourage her to copy you. She will love the new noises you make.

♪ Lullaby playlist

Download some free nursery songs and lullabies from internet websites and put together a musical compilation you can play to your baby when you need to be hands-free to finish a chore or get ready to leave the house. You may want to make up playlists for different moods: pick out a soothing lullaby collection that will help him settle down, so he gradually starts to recognize it as a cue for a quiet time; and a series of upbeat, happy songs that will make him kick his legs with excitement. Play the compilations often so your baby gets to know them well. And, since another voice is singing the songs and lullabies, you will get a bit of a break from singing to him yourself all day!

Look-up tummy time

Put your baby on his front on a soft rug for some tummy time. Lie down on your stomach in front of him so that your heads are almost touching and together you form a long line. Encourage him to lift his head and push up with his arms by holding a toy just in front of him and slightly above his head so he has to look up. This game is a helpful building block for him learning how to start crawling later on.

Make an
energy-boosting
smoothie

Your baby needs all your energy and attention, so if you find yourself flagging make yourself a nutrient-rich smoothie to boost your vitality. It's quick and easy to make, and can be adapted to suit your tastes. Use approximately 5 fl oz (150 ml) plain yogurt—or a nut milk such as almond milk, or rice or oat milk—as a basic ingredient. Include a few nuts or seeds (sunflower, sesame, and pumpkin work well) for essential fatty acids, toasted oat flakes if you want a more filling drink, and lemon or lime juice if you want a zing. Add fresh fruit and vegetables of your choice and purée in a food processor until the mixture is free of lumps. Add some apple juice if the smoothie is very thick.

Some good combinations include: equal quantities of orange and carrot juice with fresh mango and a little fresh ginger; one apple, ½ cucumber, and a small handful of fresh mint leaves; or ½ avocado, a small handful of watercress, a few fresh mint leaves, and 3½ fl oz (100 ml) apple juice.

What type of
family are you?

Four months is a good moment to think about what kind of parents you want to be—for example, whether you like routines or prefer to take the day as it comes. Audit the first few months of your baby's life and see what has worked well and what has been less successful. You may have different styles and approaches as parents, so it's a good idea to agree on the top priorities for your baby. Do you want her to go to sleep at the same time every evening no matter what; or will you keep her up to say goodnight if a working parent returns home late? Will you get a babysitter or be relaxed about taking her out with you if you go to friends' houses for dinner? Should she sleep in her own room all night or do you mind having her in your room? You may also need to decide whether to always have a calming story at bedtime rather than excited play, even if you have been at work all day and want to have some fun with her. Write down what's most important to you both and discuss how to achieve it.

Visit an
art gallery or museum

Make the most of getting out and about to places that you enjoy visiting while your baby is still very portable: put her in a carriage or front-facing baby pack and take her to an art gallery or museum. Alternatively, you might prefer to take her to a local garden center, sports event, or market. She should enjoy taking in the new environment as long as she feels secure and close to you.

He's got the whole world

Sing the song "He's got the whole world in his hands" to your baby, and then repeat it, referring to your family members, and any pets, if you want.

He's got the whole world in his hands,
He's got the whole world in his hands,
He's got the whole world in his hands,
He's got the whole world in his hands.

He's got the tiny little baby in his hands...
...He's got the whole world in his hands

He's got you and me, brother...

He's got everybody here...

Make a
splash

If you are moving your baby to a full-size family bathtub, make sure you have a couple of floating toys—rubber ducks are fun—to encourage her to kick her legs and splash the water while you support her neck and back with your hand and forearm.

Introduce family
traditions

Think about which family traditions you would like to establish. Whether it's a custom from your own family heritage or a new one you're making up for yourselves, these will become the fabric of your family life for many years. For example, some families buy their children a new decoration to hang on a Christmas tree every year, others might gather children to spin a Dreidel on Hanukkah or help cook for a Kwanzaa feast. You may want to establish family cuddle time for half an hour in bed on a weekend morning before getting up, going for a relaxed walk, or turning off the TV or radio on a Sunday evening to play games outside in good weather or indoors when it's colder.

Afternoon walk

Festive customs

Connect with cousins

Saturday playtime

MONTH 4

Sunday snuggles

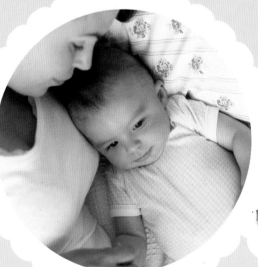

Family games

Visual discovery

Look for some bright, everyday objects around the house—
such as a large ball of yarn, a colorful hairbrush, and a few boldly
patterned items you may have. Hold each object in turn about
12 in (30 cm) away from your baby's face and explain what they
are to her. Let her explore
them with her eyes.

Busy bee

With your baby in your arms,
hold your finger up, move it
around in the air, and make a
buzzing noise. Her eyes should
follow your finger. Land the "bee" on
her skin with a slight tickle, and repeat
several times. Then hold her finger in the
air and move it around as you make the
buzzing noise. Land her finger
on your cheek and
express enough
surprise to
make her
laugh.

Try a simple
clapping song

Clapping is a complicated movement for a baby, involving motor control and good timing to bring both palms together in front of her body. Although she won't master it until she's a few months older, she will love to watch how you clap to a beat as you repeat this rhyme to her:

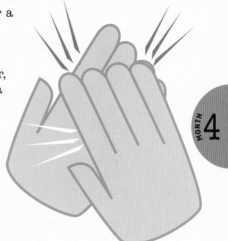

Patty-cake, patty-cake, baker's man,
Bake me a cake as fast as you can;
Pat it, and roll it, and mark it with a "B,"
And put it in the oven for baby and me.

MONTH 4

Smell new scents

Your baby has a growing ability to tell the difference between smells. See if she reacts to a variety of scents as you present them to her. Try holding a vanilla pod, then a whole nutmeg seed, a jar of cloves, a sprig each of rosemary and lavender, and a fragrant flower in blossom close to her nose.

Your baby at...
4-5 months

Everything you do with your baby helps him to **discover more** about his world. He's beginning to understand *cause* and *effect* when he **shakes a rattle** and it **makes a noise**, and *anticipate* a **surprise** when you play peekaboo. He will also love the **excitement** of hearing and watching you sing familiar *clapping songs* and *rhymes*. He may **enjoy** looking at more **complex patterns** now, and will *listen* carefully to the **sounds** you make as you **talk to him**.

by this age
your baby is probably able to:

✿ Discover the concept of cause and effect when his actions make something happen

✿ Anticipate what happens next in familiar rhymes or action games

✿ Make more repetitive sounds

✿ Enjoy exploring different textures

✿ Occasionally surprise himself by rolling over from his tummy onto his back when he reaches for something

✿ Push up with his arms

Some babies may even be able to:
✿ Rock back and forth on their tummies

The art of
anticipation

Your baby is now at a great age to enjoy some interactive songs. The repetitive words and rhythms are good for her language development, and she will love anticipating the movements you make with her as you say or sing each rhyme. The actions will also help her use her limbs and improve her motor skills. Keep eye contact with her at all times so she can catch your sense of fun as she watches you.

Humpty Dumpty

Sit your baby on a soft surface, propping her up against some cushions if she needs support, and sit facing her, or sit her on your lap facing you. Hold her hands, or hold her under her armpits, and as Humpty falls, let her lean back gently while keeping hold of her.

Humpty Dumpty sat on a wall,
Humpty Dumpty had a great fall.
All the king's horses and all the king's men
Couldn't put Humpty together again.

The grand
old Duke of York

Either lie on the floor with your knees bent, feet resting on the floor, and your baby sitting on your abdomen, or sit with your back supported and your baby on your lap facing you. Hold her firmly around her middle with your hands and raise her up in the air and lower her down as you sing about marching up and down:

Oh, the grand old Duke of York,
He had ten thousand men;
He marched them up to the top of the hill,
And he marched them down again.

And when they were up, they were up,
And when they were down, they were down,
And when they were only half-way up,
They were neither up nor down.

Jack and Jill
go up the hill

Sit with your back supported and your knees up with your baby on your lap facing you. In this position you can support her body as you gently bring her up and down. Gently tip to one side together as you finish.

Jack and Jill went up the hill,
To fetch a pail of water.
Jack fell down,
And broke his crown.
And Jill came tumbling after!

Footprint plaque

As a permanent reminder of your baby's early months, make a 3D impression of his feet (or hands). Use a plaster cast kit or buy extra-light, air-dry white clay from an art or craft store, or online, to create a keepsake for yourselves, or to give away as a gift to grandparents. If you don't get a good set of imprints the first time, just reroll the clay and try again.

1

5 MONTH

Roll out the clay to a thickness of ¼ in (5 mm) on a flat clean surface using a rolling pin. Use an upturned bowl and a knife to cut a circle.

2

Put the clay circle on a plate. Hold your baby over the plate and press his feet, one at a time, into the clay to get an even imprint of each sole and all his toes.

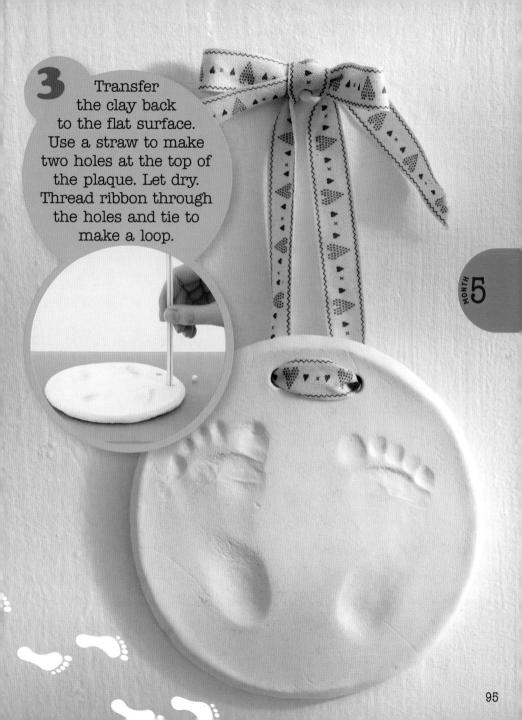

3 Transfer the clay back to the flat surface. Use a straw to make two holes at the top of the plaque. Let dry. Thread ribbon through the holes and tie to make a loop.

Social baby

At this age your baby will enjoy seeing your friends almost as much as you do. So, while she is still very portable, arrange to meet some friends during the day and bring her along. You may want to make a lunch date with a couple of friends from work on their lunch break, or brunch with a group of old friends on the weekend, for example. Turn the get-together into a reason for an adventurous trip on the bus or train. And the more attention your baby receives from your friends, the better!

Playback

Your baby is using her voice—plus movements and expressions—to make herself understood. It's important to keep repeating the sounds she makes back to her to encourage her to listen and make more sounds, and explore using her voice. For a change, why not record her babblings and cooings on your smart phone or computer. You could try tickling her toes to make her giggle too. Then play the recording back to her several times, telling her that it is her who is talking.

Grab and scrunch

As she grows more confident grabbing and holding onto objects, your baby is ready to explore more unusual items that make a noise. Crumple up a large piece of brown or wax paper and pass it to her to grab and scrunch. She should be fascinated by the noises she makes as she wraps her fingers around the crinkly paper.

Go on a
nature trail

Carry your baby around your yard or take her to a local woodland or park to introduce her to a wealth of new experiences, with all kinds of smells, sights, and sounds to take in. Talk about what you can see and hear as you walk; look up at a butterfly, get down low to study a snail, touch the delicate petals of a flower and a rough tree trunk, and smell pine cones and herbs.

Feed the ducks

Take a trip to your nearest pond or river to feed the ducks. Although your baby is still too young to feed the birds himself, he is now at a good age to concentrate longer, see the ducks clearly and track their movements, and be completely engaged by their noisy quacking. As you feed them, you might want to say a couple of verses from the rhyme "Five little ducks":

Five little ducks
Went out one day
Over the hill and far away.
Mother duck said,
"Quack, quack, quack, quack."
But only four little ducks came waddling back.

Four little ducks...
Three little ducks...
Two little ducks...
One little duck... but no little ducks came waddling back.

Sad mother duck
Went out one day
Over the hill and far away.
The sad mother duck said,
"Quack, quack, quack, quack."
And five little ducks came waddling back.

Make an extra large family photo album

At around five months your baby is becoming more interested in socializing, and is quite happy to be entertained by other people as long as you stay nearby. To help him become more familiar with faces other than your own, enlarge some photos of family members and friends who he sees more regularly. Cut out images of their faces, as well as your own baby's face, and stick them into a large notebook. Look through the book together and talk about the different faces and who they belong to.

MONTH 5

Try these...

All change

It may only take seconds for your happy, smiling baby to become fretful and cry, especially if she is overtired or has had too much excitement. Respond by quickly changing the pace. Simply producing a book or turning on some calming music, for example, will help you instantly create a quieter atmosphere and you can then soothe her further with some gentle snuggle time together.

Try a toy that lights up

Your baby's hand control may be improving rapidly now, and she will want to try to swipe at or grab all kinds of objects that come within reach. Appropriate toys for this stage include any that are easy to grip—and if the toy lights up, it will appear even more attractive to her. See if you can borrow, trade, or buy a toy with colorful elements that light up; she will be intrigued to try to hold and explore it.

Keep hugging

It's never too early to teach your baby how to give and receive affection. You're already the best role model for her by hugging and kissing her, but this time you give her a hug, say, "You hug me," and see if she can hug you back. If your baby is not a natural hugger, show her gentle affection at a level that she can respond to.

Change of face

Now that your baby is enjoying looking at new faces and responding to their smiles and conversation, invite friends and relatives over for coffee to widen her social circle. While they are with you, ask if they want to sing her a favorite song or rhyme to let her hear familiar sounds from someone different.

Game of soccer

Watch a soccer game together in the park or at a local sports center: sit your baby on your knee and watch the game for a little while, pointing out where the ball is to help her eyes focus and track the movement. Also talk about the players and how they move around.

Diaper-free time

Don't forget to give your baby the freedom to kick and wiggle without a diaper on. Being diaper-free means she is able to improve aspects of her coordination, such as bringing her toes to her mouth. It's also good for her skin, too. Put her on a soft washable rug, make sure the room temperature is warm, and let her play.

What happens next?

MONTH 5

Now that your baby is beginning to anticipate what happens next when you say or do something, tell her what you are going to do before you do it. For example, say, "I'm going to pick you up now," then stretch out your arms to her.

Natural mimic

You are still your baby's favorite play thing and she increasingly wants to imitate you, so keep talking expressively to her as you do your daily chores and activities together, and give her space to try to respond to you. Let her hold a clean cloth so she can copy you as you wipe down a table or her high chair, for example. Tell her what you are doing and see if she will babble in reply.

Name check

Your baby is learning quickly and in the next few months she will begin to recognize her own name. Start to use her name frequently now and she'll soon know you mean her.

Where's bear?

Place a teddy bear or a favorite toy in a paper bag inside a small cardboard box. Put the box in a paper bag. You can even add a couple more layers, if you want. Ask your baby where the teddy bear is as you unwrap each layer, and let him reach for his bear as you open the paper bag.

place your hands over your baby's

Ready to clap

To help your baby get used to clapping, try a new clapping song such as "If you're happy and you know it, clap your hands." When you repeat the song, place your hands gently over his and bring them together. You'll be helping him practice his gross and fine motor control and rhythm.

Draw your
baby's family tree

Help to strengthen your baby's sense of belonging by creating a big
family tree to look at together. Draw a large colorful picture of a tree
and stick photographs of close family members onto it. Hang it on his
nursery wall or in the kitchen and hold him in your arms to look at it
together. It will also act as another way of bonding with grandparents,
aunts and uncles, siblings, and cousins.

grandparents

dad

mom

brother

you

sister

103

Introducing "in" and "out"

Although this will become a favorite game when your baby is a little older, now is a good time to introduce the idea of in and out to her. Sit together with a basket containing a few of her favorite toys in front of you. Pull out each toy and say "Out!" When the basket is empty, reverse the process, saying "In!" as you put each toy back. Give her a chance to explore each toy as you go.

Take peekaboo to a new dimension

In addition to playing peekaboo by hiding your face behind your hands or a baby blanket, try partially hiding your baby's face under the blanket for a second or two. Then lift the material and exaggerate your surprised response as you say "Boo!" You may want to try the same approach with a favorite toy or larger stuffed animal: partially hide it under the baby blanket and then express surprise to see the toy peeking out. Point it out and say, "There's the toy!" Her love of repetition means this game can go on and on!

Roly-poly game

You'll notice your baby's head control is well-established, her neck and arm muscles are getting stronger, and she may be practicing the moves that help her to roll over. Lie her on her tummy on a rug and put a toy down just in front of her and slightly to one side. As she reaches for it, she may get closer to rolling over or surprise herself by actually doing it. Praise her if she does, since she may be a little surprised to find herself upside down. Gently guide her back onto her tummy and see if she wants to try the game again.

MONTH 5

Try larger board books

Now that your baby's concentration skills are improving, look for some bigger board books with very colorful pictures and more detail to add new visual stimulation when you have story time together.

Play the
name
game

At this stage, naming everything you show your baby is helping him begin to develop the association between an object and the word we use to label it. As you name objects—even everyday items such as a sun hat or spoon—he's taking in vital information to support his language development by looking at the shape of your mouth, your facial expression, and the sound of the word.

5 MONTH

"Cup"

Take three familiar objects and put them in front of your baby. Ask him, "Where is your rattle?" Then pick up the rattle and give it to him, saying, "Here is your rattle." Repeat with the other objects. Look for a new combination of items every time you play the game.

"Puppet"

"Car"

Start
naming colors

Your baby's eyesight is developing, so start naming colors as you play. Make a simple tower with three or four colored blocks, naming each color as you pile them up. Then let her enjoy knocking them down with your help.

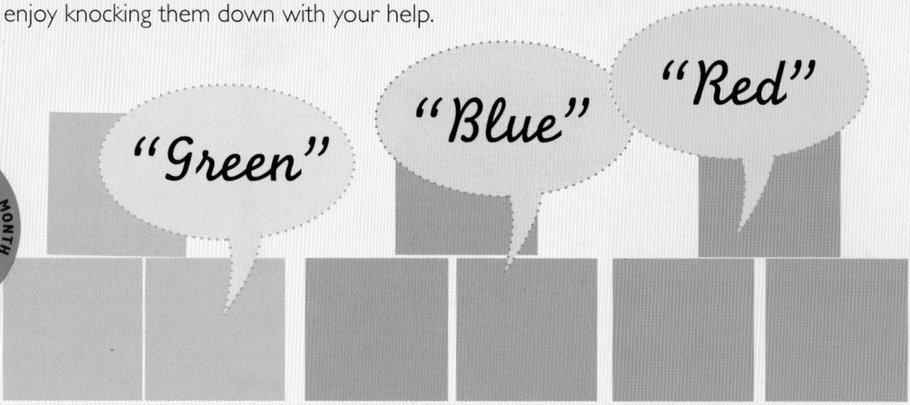

5 MONTH

"Green"

"Blue"

"Red"

Have a change of scene

A quick change of scene can help to alter the mood or break up a long day. Whether it's raining or not, take a short walk outside under an umbrella together. Or just walk to the street to watch people go by and wave to any familiar faces. If you have a local corner store and have run out of something, a quick trip there can give purpose to your excursion.

Enjoy some
downtime together

Play some calming classical or instrumental music for a short while every day. Choose something restful and with a slower beat, such as slow jazz or a gentle piano or flute concerto. Or try meditative music like Celtic or Indian flute. Making this part of your routine—maybe after you have fed your baby—will give you both a chance to rest, avoid overstimulation, and enjoy being close as you listen to the music.

Bumping
noses

Hold your baby in your arms. Whisper "Boo!" and move your head toward her. Say "Boo!" quietly and move your head even closer. Say "Boo!" a little louder (but don't shout!) and bump noses gently. She should love watching your face up close and enjoy the fun tone in your voice.

Your baby at...

5–6 months

Your baby's brain is *developing* at the fastest rate it ever will as his **awareness** of the world develops. His *language skills* are **improving** as you keep eye-to-eye contact with him, **point out** things to him, **describe** them, and **repeat** yourself. He will also start to **experiment** with *vowel sounds*. As his *physical strength* improves, he may also be preparing to *sit up unaided*.

by this age
your baby is probably able to:

🌸 Roll over from his front onto his back

🌸 Reach for toys he wants

🌸 Concentrate for short periods

🌸 Hold out his arms if he wants to be picked up

🌸 Give and receive affection

🌸 Start practising basic sounds such as "ga, ga" and "ka, ka"

Some babies may even be able to:

🌸 Combine vowels and consonants to say, for example, "ah-goo"

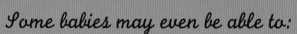

Bath-time fun!

If your baby
has made the transition from a baby
bath to a real bathtub, bath time can be a highlight of
his day. Let him discover a greater sense of freedom as he
splashes in the water and explores different sensations.

Keep some favorite bath toys on hand (you don't need to buy special bath
toys; nonbattery plastic toys you may already have will work well). Try playing
different games and activities, such as a tickle game: use a hand puppet washcloth
or sponge to tickle his toes, knees, and tummy. Or sing a familiar rhyme or silly
song and splash the surface water lightly as you sing. Supervise him carefully at all
times while he's in or near the water.

If your baby shows signs of apprehension or dislikes this bigger
environment, make it as fun and relaxing as possible—or jump in and
join him in the bath.

6 MONTH

Bubbles
in the bath

Add a little bubble bath appropriate for children's sensitive skin as the bath runs. Once he's in the water, gently blow some of the bubbly froth onto his tummy. Then bury a bath toy under the foam to discover together. Using a large wand, blow some big bubbles and let them pop on his fingers or nose.

MONTH 6

Squirty
water

If you have a plastic funnel or sieve and a clean, empty dish soap bottle, bring them to the bathroom with you. Half-fill the bottle with water and gently squirt it into the bath, or pour water through the funnel or sieve onto your baby's feet so he can kick and giggle at the sensation.

Change the
scenery

Your baby will enjoy looking up at something different in her sleeping area, especially if she has had the same decorations since she was born, or if you are thinking of moving her into her own bedroom. Make colorful bunting to brighten up the walls and window (make sure that she can't reach the bunting).

1

Draw a flag template on tracing paper and cut it out. Pin the template onto some patterned fabric and cut out two flag shapes.

2

Pin the fabric cutouts together, with the wrong side of the material facing out. Repeat steps 1 and 2 to make as many flags as you need.

3 Sew the long sides of each flag together and turn the flag the right way around, leaving a ½ in (1 cm) seam allowance. Trim the fabric edges with pinking shears.

4 Insert the flags into a folded length of bias tape, and pin. Leave a 2 in (5 cm) gap between each flag. Sew the flags and folded bias in place.

MONTH 6

115

Go to the ZOO

Your baby is so curious about his surroundings and is very receptive to new experiences. Take a trip to a local zoo or petting zoo and make the appropriate noises for each animal as you watch them. When you get home, look at pictures of the animals and repeat the noises, or sing the rhyme "Old MacDonald's Farm" while you play with a set of toy farm animals together.

Start swimming

Pick a quiet time of day to take your baby for her first swim, or sign up for parent and baby classes. Check beforehand that the pool isn't too chilly; ideally it should be 86° F/30° C or more. Having fun kicking and splashing around in your arms helps her to work a lot of muscles. It's also a great way to wear her out if she's very active, and may even help her sleep well!

Apple fingers

Dab a little unsweetened apple purée onto each of your baby's fingers and encourage him to lick it all off. Count off each finger aloud as he sucks off the purée.

Bubble bottle

Half-fill a small plastic water bottle with water, and add a few drops of dish-washing liquid and food coloring. Screw the lid back on very firmly. Shake the bottle, give it to your baby to hold and watch colored bubbles appear inside the bottle. You can also roll it along the floor and watch the bubbles form, or use it as a bath time toy.

Arrange a toy swap

Get together with a couple of good friends and regularly trade the toys you have to give your baby fresh stimulation—or search out a toy library, which can often be found at local libraries and children's centers, to borrow new toys.

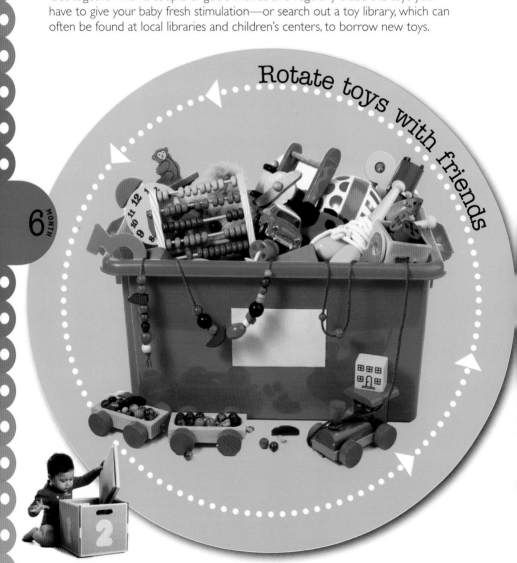

Rotate toys with friends

6 MONTH

Pelvic lifts
with baby on board

If it's becoming harder to find time to tone up now that your baby is more active, try this exercise. She should enjoy lying on your lap and being lifted up and down as you tone your abdominal and leg muscles and improve the flexibility of your spine.

1 **Lie on your back on a mat** or nonslip surface with your knees bent and feet slightly apart. Sit your baby on your abdomen, let her rest against your thighs, and hold her around her arms or middle. As you exhale, lift your pelvis slightly off the floor, hold briefly, then inhale and lower. Repeat 10 times.

2 **If you want to work harder,** exhale and lift your pelvis right off the floor so your torso and thighs are in a straight line. Hold briefly, then inhale and lower your pelvis to the floor. Keep talking to your baby the whole time to engage her attention. Repeat as many times as you can.

Try these...

One too many

Place three small toys or colorful blocks your baby can hold in his hands in front of him. Hand one to your baby, and then another so his hands are full. Then offer him the third toy or block so he has to decide which object to drop in order to take the third one.

Make a father's or mother's day gift

Put together a gift from your baby for your partner: record his babbles or giggles as a ringtone on their phone, or have a photo of your family printed on a mug or canvas bag, for example. Or just make a simple homemade card with your baby's photo on the front.

Daily read

Paste a photo of your baby onto a sheet of paper. Stick a few images from magazines of familiar objects or activities—a car, food, other babies, toys—around the photo with poster putty, and point to them as you describe them to him. Change the images as often as you look at them.

Have a play date at home

If your baby is shy and finds baby and toddler groups overwhelming, invite a parent and their baby over to give him a calmer social experience. Set your babies down together on a rug with some toys; they will probably watch and even copy each other as they play their own games.

The wheels on the bus

Sing the song "The wheels on the bus" to your baby and then take a bus ride together and sing the song again as you travel. Whisper it into his ear if you don't want to be overheard.

Mirrored action song

Sit on the floor with your baby facing you. Clap your hands, stamp your feet, pat your head, and so on as he watches you, and see if he can mirror your actions. Guide his hands and feet if he needs some help.

Yes and no

Introduce the idea of yes and no. If your baby is reaching out for a hug, smile and say "Yes." If he does something you don't like or that's not safe, frown and say "No."

Jack-in-the-box

Make a Jack-in-the-box to entertain your baby. Use a pencil to make a small hole in the base of a styrofoam cup. Push a straw through the hole. Attach a finger puppet to the top of the straw. Push the straw up and down so the puppet peeps out of the cup and say, "Hello!"

Play the
pots and pans

Once she's sitting upright, let your baby try some noisy games such as banging upside down pots and pans with a wooden or plastic spoon, whisk, or even a rattle. Show her how to bang the pan and then let her discover how to make sounds herself.

Dropping
game

Gather up some small soft toys that are easy for your baby to grasp. Find a plastic beach bucket or bowl, sit your baby next to it, catch her attention, and then drop each toy into the bucket from a height. Say "Oops" as each object drops and then ask her if she can reach into the bucket for the toy and grab it.

Who's that baby?

Hang a large unbreakable mirror in front of your baby so she can sit and look into it—or sit her on your lap and hold the mirror in front of her. As she looks into the mirror at her own reflection, point to the different parts of her face and name them. She will be intrigued by what she sees, even though she won't recognize her own face yet.

Boomerang toy

Your baby's hand–eye coordination can benefit from looking up at moving objects and trying to grab them. Tie a lightweight soft toy to a length of strong elastic and bounce it up and down in front of her, adding "boing'" noises as it boomerangs back to her. Let her track the toy with her eyes and try to grab and hold on to it to sustain her interest.

Messy play

Combine 2 cups of cornstarch with approximately 1 cup of water and a few drops of natural food coloring to make a gloppy mixture that your baby can get messy with. Sit him in his high chair with a bib on, put the mixture on the tray, and let him spread it around with his hands. You may want to use a spoon to put some of the glop onto the palms of his hands so he can feel the sensation of it oozing through his fingers.

Shadow show

Shine a flashlight against a wall in a dimly lit room. Make shapes with your hands to create simple animal shadows as you tell your baby a short story.

Screen scream!

A movie theater in your area may have special movie screenings for parents or caregivers and babies on weekdays. See if your baby will happily sit or sleep on your lap as you watch the movie. He may even be entranced by the images on the large screen, or the music. Or try taking him to a puppet show for toddlers instead: as he sits in the audience, he's having his first experience of live theater.

Exploring
taste and texture

Your baby's busy mouthing everything he holds onto. Collect a frozen teething ring, and some safe objects—perhaps a wooden spoon, spatula, a few toys, and small peeled banana—pop them in a mixing bowl, and sit with him while he brings each object to his mouth to explore it. Explain to him what he is holding and how it feels or tastes as you watch him react to the objects with different facial expressions.

Give your baby
a massage

This is a perfect age for your baby to enjoy a gentle massage on her head, tummy, and limbs, perhaps as part of her bedtime routine after a bath. This calm, soothing way of bonding together will also help her to relax and release tension before she sleeps. Keep the room warm and use a plant-based or edible oil such as olive oil (see p22). As you massage her with gentle, unrushed strokes, keep her attention by singing a lullaby or calmly whispering loving words to her.

Head and tummy

Lie your baby on her back on a soft towel. Start by stroking her head with your hands. Then massage her forehead, working from the center out. Move your fingers over her eyebrows and cheeks and out toward her ears. Then stroke the sides of her face with your thumbs.

Move your hands down to her chest and spread them out to the sides of her rib cage. Without lifting your hands, bring them back round in a circular motion to the center of her chest.

Legs and feet

Massage one leg at a time, working from the thigh down. Gently stroke and squeeze the leg as you work down to the foot. Finish by very gently pulling her leg and foot through your hands. Hold her feet and rub the soles with your thumbs, then gently pull each of her toes with your finger and thumb.

Arms and hands

Massage one arm at a time, working from the top of her arm down to her fingers. Then gently stroke and squeeze each arm with your hand. Rub the palms of her hands with your thumbs and very gently pull each of her fingers with your finger and thumb.

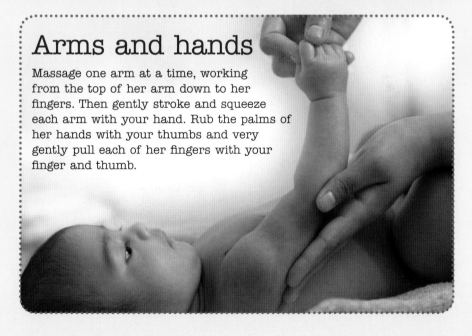

Form an impromptu band

Get the family or some of your friends to join you in grabbing a range of instant instruments—a pan and spoon, a trumpet made of rolled-up paper, a whistle, and so on—and give your baby a rattle to hold. Give a performance of favorite songs, singing them in silly voices as you play your instruments, dancing around the living room, and trying to make him laugh.

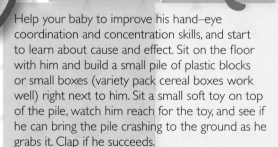

All fall down

Help your baby to improve his hand–eye coordination and concentration skills, and start to learn about cause and effect. Sit on the floor with him and build a small pile of plastic blocks or small boxes (variety pack cereal boxes work well) right next to him. Sit a small soft toy on top of the pile, watch him reach for the toy, and see if he can bring the pile crashing to the ground as he grabs it. Clap if he succeeds.

Tickly toes

Pour a layer of fine sand into a deep-sided tray or baking sheet and hold your baby over it so his feet are touching the sand tray. Trickle sand over his toes and let him move his feet around for lots of tactile stimulation.

MONTH 6

Where, oh where...

Say this rhyme to help your baby begin to identify more parts of his body. Touch the different parts as you name them:

Where, oh where, are your little fingers?
Where, oh where, are your tiny toes?
Where, oh where, is your belly button?
Round and round it goes.

Where, oh where, are your two small ears?
And where, oh where, is your nose?
Where, oh where, is your belly button?
Round and round it goes.

6–7 months

Your six-month-old is developing **new skills** as he gains **more control over his body** and his reflexes drop away. His improving *strength* and *coordination skills* mean that he may now be *sitting upright* and even preparing to **crawl**, and he is beginning to use *arm gestures* to make himself understood. He is now **refining** *his senses* of **touch, sight, taste, hearing,** and **smell.** He is more **self-aware,** and he is thriving on *repetition* to consolidate his learning.

by this age

your baby is probably able to:

* ✿ Hold his head steady

* ✿ Enjoy sitting up unsupported

* ✿ Chuckle

* ✿ Alter his tone of voice to express himself

* ✿ Make sounds and bang objects to attract your attention

* ✿ Develop his understanding of cause and effect

* ✿ Use arm gestures, such as lifting his arms for a cuddle

Some babies may even be able to:

* ✿ Try to pick up food to feed themselves or hold a sippy cup

Animal magic

Visit friends who own pets if you don't have your own, so your baby can watch the animals closely from the safety of your arms, hear the noises they make, and become familiarized with them so he's not easily scared. A visit to a petting zoo or educational farm is another good way of introducing him to animals. Explain the importance of always asking to pet an animal before touching it so he understands good pet manners from an early age.

Dance
to different tunes

Select a playlist of different songs, hold your baby carefully in your arms, and dance together. Sway to slow music, march to a strong drumming beat, and bounce up and down to exuberant music.

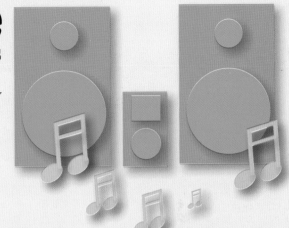

Whirling
toy windmill

Blow on a brightly colored windmill so it whirls around to capture your baby's attention. He may want to help you hold the handle while you blow and watch the colors on the wheel blur.

Jell-O hands

Your baby's grasping reflex, concentration skills, and hand–eye coordination may all be improving now. She's figuring out how to grab and grip objects, bring them up to her mouth to explore them further, and pass them from one hand to another. Jell-O is a wonderful ingredient with which to practice all these skills: she can squish, swirl, squeeze, and taste the mixture and enjoy some messy playtime.

Mandarin Jell-O

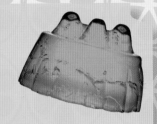

Use some of this tasty, naturally sweet gelatin for your baby to play with (left), and save the rest for desserts; it will keep in the fridge for up to 48 hours if you cover it in non-PVC plastic wrap. Makes 6 baby portions.

ingredients
10½oz (300 g) can mandarin oranges in fruit juice
¼oz (8 g) or 1 heaping tsp unflavored gelatin
unsweetened orange juice

method
1 Drain the fruit from the can and reserve the juice. Transfer the fruit to a shallow dish.

2 Put 3 tablespoons of very hot, but not boiling, water in a small bowl and sprinkle the gelatin over it. Let stand for 5 minutes, then stir the mixture until the gelatin has completely dissolved.

3 Pour the reserved juice into a measuring cup and add the gelatin and enough orange juice to make 10 fl oz (300 ml). Pour the gelatin mixture into the dish of fruit and refrigerate until it is set.

Continue your journey together

Keep up with your childbirth group by taking it to the next stage; why not try to catch up once a month, perhaps, and put the dates into the calendar. Some parents still arrange get-togethers 20 years later to share stories of family life. Since the children are the same age and have known each other since birth, both children and parents share deep ties.

If you want the rest of the family to join in, arrange to meet on weekends. You may all want to gather in the park for a picnic in the warmer months, or organize a potluck lunch for the adults at someone's house, and give your babies their own lunches together first.

Add to your repertoire

Your baby loves repetition, but he'll also enjoy new songs and poems now. If you want to add to your range of familiar nursery rhymes or change them—perhaps with some multicultural and modern verses—search online for new rhymes to bring yourself up to date. There is a wealth of online resources available, many with short videos so you can learn the tune and actions as well as the words. Enjoy practicing them together.

Set the alarm

If your baby is now in a regular sleeping routine, you may have more energy during the day. When he is down to sleep it's tempting to catch up on email or household chores; this can be unavoidable, but set an alarm on your phone to stop after 15 or 20 minutes and have some down time to relax so you are both refreshed when he wakes.

Balancing on a ball

At this age babies have to look at their hands to know where to put them; later on, once they are spatially aware, they don't need to check first by looking. Balancing your baby on a ball promotes his spacial awareness by providing feedback to his brain to tell him where he is in space. Hold him securely face down on his tummy on an aerobic or stability ball (available inexpensively online or from a sports store, or use a toy ball hopper). Gently tip him from side to side and backward and forward on the ball, making encouraging noises as you do so.

Name familiar
sounds

Help your baby to listen and become aware of the different sounds in her immediate environment. As you move around the house, name the sound you can hear, ask your baby if she can hear the noise, and point to the source as you name it. Indoor sounds can include running water from a faucet, the telephone ringing, footsteps on the sidewalk outside, a bus passing by, and the doorbell ringing. When you go outside, listen for the sounds of birds singing, airplanes and trains going by, children playing, dogs barking, and leaves on the trees rustling in the wind.

Start a news book

A notebook containing daily news about your baby is a wonderful way of keeping track of all the small but significant developments in her everyday life. It's also a lovely record to share at the end of the day with your partner if one or both of you have been out at work or away from your baby for any length of time. Describe any activities your little one has enjoyed or encountered for the first time and her reactions to different situations, objects, people, food, and so on.

You may also want to take pictures on your phone of any memorable outings, playdates, and milestones.

MONTH 7

Try these...

Your baby learns how to relate to others by watching what you do, so you are his first role model. Exaggerate your words and actions when you say please and thank you to him, and make a point of waiting your turn to speak, to show him the right way to behave and interact with other people.

Round and round the garden

Humpty Dumpty with actions

Lie on your back on a rug on a grassy lawn outdoors or a soft carpet indoors with your knees raised and your baby on your tummy. Repeat the rhyme "Humpty Dumpty" to him and roll gently onto your side so he slides to the floor as Humpty falls.

Say the rhyme "Round and round the garden" to your baby as you trace a circle on his hand or tummy with your finger, and finish with a big tickle to make him laugh:

Round and round the garden
Like a teddy bear.
One step, two steps,
And tickle him under there!

Airplanes

Your baby's neck muscles are strong enough for him to "fly." Lie on your back on the floor, knees bent, with him sitting on your tummy facing you. Place your hands firmly around his middle. Ask him, "Are we ready to fly?" Count to three, slowly lift him up in the air above you, move him around a little in several different directions, and make lots of airplane noises. Then lower him back down.

Back and forth

Now that your baby is sitting upright more often, sit together on the floor facing each other. Roll a soft ball toward him and encourage him to push or bat the ball back to you with his hands.

Include yourself in photos

Don't forget to take photos of yourself with your baby to record many moments spent together in his young life. If you don't have a smartphone or a camera function for taking self-portraits, ask friends, family, or even a passer-by, to take a photo of you both.

Mini gym crawl

If your baby is starting to roll, bottom-shuffle, or crawl, get down next to him and move around on the floor together. Your baby will try to copy you, but you can also copy him and turn the activity into a fun mini gym session.

MONTH 7

Pass the ball

Take a soft ball or fluffy pom-pom (see p159) and demonstrate how you can pass it between your hands and to your baby. Encourage him to try to pass it back to you.

Sing in a silly voice

Sing familiar action songs such as "Old MacDonald had a farm" in silly accents and different voices—high, squeaky, or very soft right into your baby's ear— to make him giggle and help him to develop a sense of anticipation as he waits to see what you will do next.

Take a texture
trip

Walk around the house with your baby looking for objects with texture: a soft carpet, cool fridge, hard floor, fluffy towel, furry toy, smooth cushion, silky scarf, and so on. Let her feel the objects as you name and describe them.

Water play

If it's warm outside, sit your baby on the grass or a mat in front of a plastic tub or bowl with a little lukewarm water—or dig out her old baby bath. If it's cold outside, lay some newspaper or a waterproof mat on the floor indoors. Add a few plastic cups or measuring spoons, or plastic bath toys, and pour in a little child-friendly bubble bath if you want bubbles in the bowl too. Show her how to practice her hand–eye coordination by patting the surface of the water with her hands and picking up the objects.

Felt board story time

Cover a large board in bright felt and stick or staple the edges in place on the back of the board. Buy or cut out and make your own colorful felt shapes—sea creatures, animals, figures or faces, plants, and insects—and press them onto the felt board; the fabric will naturally stick to itself. Tell your baby a simple story using the different pieces.

Treasure basket

Collect a variety of safe objects from around the house—a spatula, a few colorful blocks, a soft toy or two, and a couple of plastic bowls, for example—and store them in a basket or box that is easy to reach. When you sit down with your baby, pull an object from the basket and describe what it is. Then let him explore what else is in the basket.

Bath time foam blocks

During bath time, float some brightly colored foam sponges or dense foam blocks on the water. Push them down beneath the water and exclaim with surprise as they pop back up. See if your baby can help you push the foam back down.

Ask direct questions

When you talk to your baby and ask him something, slow your speech down and emphasize certain words. You could ask, for example, "Do you want **juice**?" and show him his cup. Then wait for a response from him. Following a question with this quiet pause will help him learn that he needs to vocalize what he wants, and he will begin to understand that having a conversation involves taking turns.

Reverse peekaboo

Lay a light blanket or napkin over your baby's head and then express shock that he is there when you pull off the blanket. He will enjoy the element of surprising you.

Have breakfast together today

Breakfast is often the most rushed meal of the day and one that we tend to assume doesn't warrant spending time together. However, experts believe that it is important to eat meals with your baby, so try to find time to sit together at the start of the day and share a good breakfast. It will reinforce the message to her that mealtimes are social occasions.

Make some food that you can share to set you both up for the day—perhaps fruit and oats, which you soak overnight in the fridge first, French toast with fruit, biscuits with cream cheese and fruit, oatmeal with apricots (see right), or oatmeal with a few fresh or frozen raspberries stirred in. If you want the whole family to join in, plan to have breakfast together on weekends.

Apricot oatmeal

Prepare the apricot purée in advance so that the oatmeal is quick to make in the morning. If you don't have cooked apricot purée, purée some canned apricots instead.

For the apricot purée
- 3½oz (100g) fresh or dried apricots
- 8½fl oz (250ml) water

Put the apricots in a small saucepan and add the water. Cover with a lid, bring to a boil, reduce the heat, and simmer until the apricots are soft. Let cool slightly, then purée the fruit and liquid in a food processor, adding some cooled boiled water if required. Refrigerate once cooled.

For the oatmeal
- 2oz (60g) oats
- 10fl oz (300ml) whole milk

Put the oats and milk into a small saucepan and heat, stirring continuously. When the mixture thickens, remove from the heat. Keep one portion warm for yourself and cool your baby's portion to body temperature. Stir a tablespoon of apricot purée into each, and serve.

Make a
weekly survival hit list

Your busy family life will be easier to manage if you feel organized about what your baby needs each day. Plot the week ahead on a small blackboard or wipe-clean board and hang it on the kitchen door or fridge where you can see it easily. If you're starting your baby on solid food, for example, you may want to create a chart to keep track of which new foods and in what quantities you can introduce that week. Or perhaps jot down the time and date of his next playdate, or when to give him any medication he should take.

Secret treat

Show your baby a snack, cover it with a napkin, and let him discover where the snack is. If he enjoys himself while hunting for the secret treat, repeat the game, then give him the snack and encourage him to eat it.

Mirror play

To improve your baby's observation skills, stand or sit in front of a mirror with him in your arms or on your lap. Make some different expressions and funny faces. He will enjoy looking at your reflection and his (though he won't recognize himself yet) and maybe try to copy your expressions. You can also hold a favorite toy up in front of the mirror, give it a silly voice, and pretend that it is talking to him while he interacts with its reflection.

Learning to reach

Sit your baby on the floor, put a toy down just out of his reach and watch him try to stretch for it. If he becomes frustrated because he can't grab it, encourage him gently. After a few tries he should learn how to lean forward to grasp the toy. This simple game is all part of encouraging him to start crawling.

Your baby at...
7-8 months

Your baby's physical and mental skills are improving dramatically. His *hand–eye coordination* may now be sophisticated enough for him to *grab* and *grip* objects, *pass* them from **one hand** to **another**, and *put* them into a container. He still loves *repetition* and will enjoy the **simple stories** you tell him again and again. He's becoming aware of **everyday sights and sounds** around him now, too, and learning about *object permanence*.

by this age

your baby is probably able to:

❀ Clasp his hands

❀ Pass objects from hand to hand

❀ Understand object permanence – that people and objects exist even when he can't see or hear them

❀ Listen carefully when you talk to him

❀ Respond to your tone of voice

Some babies may even be able to:

❀ Push up onto their hands and knees and rock to prepare to crawl

Saying hello
for the first time

If you meet people your baby doesn't know, you may find that he is shy and wants to cling to you. Although stranger anxiety is normal at this age—and may last for a couple of years—rather than force your baby to be friendly, try these simple steps:

❁ Warn your acquaintance in advance that your baby will be more comfortable if they approach him slowly and interact gently using a soft tone.

❁ Keep your baby in your arms to begin with and talk to him, explaining who the newcomer is.

❁ If your baby is sitting on the floor, suggest that the newcomer gets down on his level and passes him a favorite toy to build a sense of familiarity.

❁ Give your baby lots of praise and encouragement if he smiles back at the newcomer.

Getting used to other babies

Your baby is fascinated by other babies and toddlers, even though at this age they will engage in parallel play rather than interact and share toys. Let him play alongside another baby or a slightly older sibling or cousin—this will help him become more social and he may gravitate toward other babies at a playgroup.

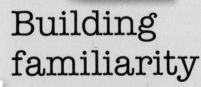

Building familiarity

You are probably out and about visiting friends and relatives now that your baby is older and more socially aware. Before you leave home, show him photos of the relatives or friends you will be visiting and repeat their names to him several times. When you are together, check that he's not overwhelmed by new people by regularly removing him for some short one-on-one time with you. Pack a comfort blanket or favorite toy in case he needs more than a hug for reassurance.

Take a train ride

Make a visit to a local train station together. Watch the trains arrive and depart, copy the noises the brakes and doors of the trains make, and talk about the people getting on and off the trains.

If it's not too far to travel, buy a ticket and take a train ride to the next station and back. Describe what you can see as you look out of the window together. Alternatively, make a pretend ticket from cardboard at home before you leave and give it to your baby to hold while you watch the trains go past.

Child Ticket

155

Try out a baby backpack carrier

Borrow or invest in a baby backpack carrier and go for a "real" walk along footpaths where you can't take a stroller; you may want to make a day trip of it and have a complete change of scenery and environment. Looking out at the world from a new perch will delight your baby. He may fall asleep in the carrier if he is soothed by the rhythm of your walking pace, which should be fine; just make sure he is wearing the backpack harness and is sleeping in a comfortable position.

Take turns

Now is a good time to help your baby learn about taking turns when you do things together. Explain to him about taking turns and say, "My turn," and "Your turn," to introduce this idea as you play. For example, let him have fun shaking a rattle or banging on a drum or upturned saucepan with a plastic drumstick or wooden spoon, and then make a point of taking a turn yourself.

You can also use this tactic to get tasks done, such as washing his face or brushing his teeth: give him a washcloth to play with and then tell him it's your turn to wipe his face.

8 MONTH

Keep emergency snacks with you

Always keep some baby-friendly snacks with you when you are out, in case your baby gets hungry and tired. Put some dried apricots, mini rice cakes, and small breadsticks in airtight Tupperware containers and keep them in the changing bag; they won't go bad or get soggy, even if you leave them in the bag for a couple of days. Keep a clean sippy cup and also a bottle of water (for you to drink from too) in your bag.

Build an obstacle course

If your baby is on the move and learning how to crawl, build a miniature obstacle course on the floor with some cushions or a beanbag and stay at ground level with him. You may want to place a toy just out of his grasp and help him clamber over the cushions to reach it if he needs encouragement to "complete" the obstacle course.

Take a mini break

If your baby is finding it hard to be separated from you, start small and make it brief: 10–15 minutes apart is a good start. This very short separation is beneficial for your baby as she learns to be away from you, and it also gives you some much-needed space to recover your energy levels a little, clear your head, and have precious time to yourself.

Give your baby to your partner, a friend, or a grandparent. Tell her that you are going and will be back soon, wave bye-bye (never sneak out), and come back when you say you will. Go into your bedroom, shut the door, and have an uninterrupted phone call with a friend, read the newspaper or a magazine, take a shower, or just relax.

Play with a
pom-pom

A simple homemade pom-pom makes a
surprisingly versatile toy. It's easy for your
baby to hold and drop to develop her grasp
reflex, it can be used as a ball, or as a texture
toy for her to explore, and it's great for tickling
too! Never leave her alone with the pom-pom.

What you need
❀ Sheet of paper
❀ Cardboard
❀ Large ball of brightly colored yarn

Draw a circle 8 in (20 cm) in diameter
on the paper. Draw a smaller circle in
the center approximately 2 in (5 cm) in
diameter (large enough to thread yarn
through). Cut out the template, place it
on the cardboard, and cut out two
disks with holes in the center.

Place the disks together. Wind the yarn
through the center of the disks and
around the outsides until they are
completely covered in yarn. Repeat at
least four times for a fluffy pom-pom.

Insert a pair of scissors between the
outside edges of the cardboard disks
and cut through the yarn.

Slide a separate length of yarn
between the disks, pull tightly around
the center of the wrapped yarn, and
secure in a firm knot. Cut away the
disks and fluff up the pom-pom.

Try these...

crunch!

Introduce books with
texture and noise

Choose a new board book with interactive elements to read to your baby. Name the textures and touch them, and name any noises as he explores the new book.

crackle!

Exaggerate
your facial expressions

As you tell your baby a story or talk about something new you will do together, make your facial expressions noticeable. He'll be studying your face as he listens to you, and it helps him to see how you are reacting.

Starring role

Make a short video recording of your baby and play it back to him so he can watch himself. He'll be intrigued, though he won't recognize himself on screen yet.

Kiss chase

Your baby is old enough to be developing a sense of anticipation now. He will love it if you stretch out your hands, warn him that you are coming to catch him, then lift him into your arms and cover him in kisses until he giggles.

Animal
diaper time

If your baby is fidgeting and frustrated during diaper changes, find large pictures of animals and stick them onto separate pieces of card. Hang one where your baby can see it as you change his diaper, and entertain him with the animal noises. Change the picture frequently. Or find large soft or plastic animals, and hand one to him during the diaper change.

This is the way...

Your baby still loves to watch what you do, even if it's a mundane task. If you brush your hair or wash your hands, for example, sing the song, "This is the way I..." as you do it. You can then repeat the song and brush your baby's hair with his brush or wipe his hands.

Learning to point

Lay your baby's soft toys in a row, point to each one with your index finger, and say what it is. Your baby may pat or wave his hand at each toy as he learns how to direct his index finger.

Open a
bank account
for your baby

If you have already received gifts of money for your baby, you may want to open a bank account for him. Take a trip to your local bank together if you want to make it a special event.

Vary story time

To keep your baby entertained, read him a familiar story in a funny voice, sing the words, or change the pace by reading one page slowly and the next fast. You can also copy things that happen to characters, like giving your baby a hug.

Baby's
first tunnel

Stand with both feet apart and give your baby lots of encouragement to shuffle or crawl between your legs. If you have a large cardboard box, open out both ends, get down at floor level with her, and show her how to crawl or roll through it. Alternatively, ask a friend or family member to rest on their hands and knees on the floor to make an arch. Crawl underneath, encourage her to follow you, and enjoy lots of laughter in the process.

8 MONTH

seek out the squeak

Your baby's hearing has been highly developed since birth, but now she may be beginning to differentiate between a variety of tones. Hide a squeaky toy or ball—or try a rattle—under a dish towel or small blanket and squeeze or shake it to give a muffled sound. Give your baby time to listen and turn to look across to where she thinks the sound is coming from, then help her find the hidden object and praise her when she uncovers the toy.

Dine
on roasted finger-foods

To make some vegetables—such as zucchini, carrots, pumpkin, parsnips, turnips, sweet potatoes, and butternut squash—more appealing for your baby to try, roast them first to increase their natural sweetness. Cut each vegetable into bite-sized pieces before roasting, and serve to your baby at room temperature.

Recipe
- Preheat the oven to 400°F (200°C).
- Wash, trim, peel if needed, and chop the vegetables into sticks about 1 in (3 cm) in length.
- Place the pieces on a baking sheet and brush lightly with a little vegetable oil.
- Bake for 20–25 minutes or until tender.
- Transfer onto some paper towels to remove any excess oil, and allow to cool.

MONTH 8

Simple
shower

Fill the container with water

Punch some holes in the lid of a plastic food container (a cottage cheese container with a tight-fitting lid is ideal) using a metal skewer. Half-fill the tub with water, replace the lid, and show your baby how to turn the tub upside down to sprinkle water over his tummy, knees, and feet. With this bath time fun, he'll be practicing his fine motor skills and learning about cause and effect.

8 MONTH

Off-peak soft play

Your baby's muscle control and coordination is increasing all the time, and he's also becoming more aware of different environments, so he may be ready to try out a soft play gym. Pick a quiet time to go—maybe during school hours, or early in the day. The ball pool is a good place to start: get in together, hold him safely in your arms, and swish him around gently.

Scrunchy sock

Stuff an old sock with scrunched-up cellophane and either tie a firm knot in the end or secure it with twine tied in a very firm knot. Show your baby how he can create scrunchy noises by squishing the sock in his hands. To turn the sock into a scrunchy snake toy, use a green sock, firmly sew a short piece of red ribbon (with a "V" shape cut out of one end to make a forked tongue), some felt eyes, and yellow felt triangles as markings along the top of the sock.

Secure the end of sock

Create your baby's
first fort

Forts will probably become a big feature of your child's imaginative play in years to come, so why not introduce him to his first fort now. Drape a sheet or tablecloth over a large table to make a hidden space, climb in together, bring a soft toy animal too, and have a pretend tea party.

Make a natural
wind chime

Being outside is wonderful for your baby because her senses will be stimulated by the different sounds, sights, and smells. Help her enjoy a new experience by making a natural wind chime and hanging it from the low branch of a tree. Stand beside it with your baby in your arms and watch how the wind rustles the chimes to produce a noise. Then show her how she can pat the chimes to create the sounds herself. You could also lie together under the tree and look up at the leaves on the branches rustling, and the wind chime swaying in the breeze, and talk about what you can see and hear.

Alternatively, you can show her how you can create rustling sounds with a pile of leaves using your hands, and watch how the leaves fall to the ground if you throw them into the air.

8 MONTH

Bamboo sticks

String

Make a shell wind chime

Twist the tip of a pair of sharp nail scissors through a shell to make a hole. Repeat with more shells, then thread them onto several lengths of string with a knot in between each shell. Secure the strings to a piece of driftwood, bamboo, or a large shell or starfish so the shells dangle down and collide as they move.

Texture play

Cold cooked noodles or large pasta pieces can make a wonderful texture "toy" for your baby to explore with his hands. He can also practice picking up the noodles or pasta with his fingers and thumbs if his pincer grip is developing. You may want to sit him in his high chair with a large mat underneath, even though this is a playtime, not a mealtime, activity. It doesn't matter if your baby eats some of the noodles or pasta while he plays.

Dinner guest

If your baby is becoming distracted and bored during mealtimes, "invite" a toy that can be wiped down to the dinner table for your baby to feed while you feed him, or for you to feed them both, and talk about his toy.

Squishy art play

Put a sheet of thick watercolor paper inside a sealable ziplock bag and drizzle a small amount of two water-based paint colors into the bag. Seal the bag properly and hand it to your baby. Show him how to press, squash, and crumple the bag, and talk about how squishy it feels and how the colors spread across the paper. When he has finished, you will have some original art to remove from the bag and allow to dry.

Play with finger people

Draw a small face on the pad of each of your fingers and thumbs with a pen. Make fists with your hands and pop up each finger in turn to say hello to your baby. Give each finger face a name and a funny voice. You can even use cotton balls as hair and fasten them in place with a dab of PVA glue.

Make up a short story about the finger characters and finish by waving both your hands at your baby and saying bye-bye.

Your baby at...
8-9 months

At around the same time that separation anxiety kicks in, your baby is becoming **more curious** about **other babies** as interesting objects and may try to *make contact* by **patting, touching,** and **babbling** at them. He can *comprehend* how objects such as a cup or hairbrush are **used,** and *understand* what the word **"no"** means. His *sense of humour* is evolving fast, as is his ability to *crawl* or bottom-shuffle!

by this age
your baby is probably able to:

❀ Develop his passing skills

❀ Understand how some objects are used

❀ Understand the word "no"

❀ Show signs of crawling

❀ Bang two objects together

❀ Respond to simple commands

❀ Copy you if you wave to him

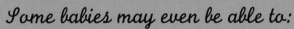

Some babies may even be able to:

❀ Pull to standing

❀ Look in the direction in which you point and make their earliest pointing gesture

Make your baby
laugh ☺

Your baby probably managed his first giggle when he was around three months old, but now that he's nine months old you might find that every so often he delights you with a great big belly laugh.

This wonderful sound is a sign that he's developing a sense of humor, and is interacting with people around him and enjoying their company. Try to figure out what tickles his funny bone.

You could:
- ✿ Make funny faces at him
- ✿ Tickle his thighs
- ✿ Pretend his feet are very, very smelly and give an enormous groan of horror.

Mood
enhancer

If you need to boost your mood, take a walk with your baby in a green space, whether it's an urban park or square, or out in the country. Although any form of exercise is a wonderful way to reach a natural "high," research shows that it takes only five minutes of "green exercise" to feel more upbeat. Your baby will also enjoy being out in the fresh air watching the world go by from his stroller.

Wave bye-bye

To help your baby get used to the idea that things come and go, wave and say, "bye-bye" whenever someone leaves, a bus moves away, or you put a soft toy back in its box. After lots of repetition with your baby watching what you say and do, he should start to respond and copy you.

Record
your baby's
development

Your baby is reaching plenty of milestones around now, so revisit her baby diary and update it by sticking in some new hand- and footprints to show how she's grown. Brush some water-based, child-friendly, nontoxic paint onto your baby's palm and press her hand down gently on watercolor paper. Repeat with the sole of her foot.

9 MONTH

Make handprint keepsakes

Why not make some extra handprints and frame them as keepsakes for yourselves and family members. Cover the backing board of each frame with some patterned fabric, fold the excess fabric over the back of the board, and fasten it with masking tape. Mount the print on the center of the fabric using double-sided tape, and then slot the board into the frame.

Frame your print and hang it on the wall

MONTH 9

Nurture your sense of humor

Your baby loves it when you make him laugh, although it can be hard to always be upbeat, especially if you're tired. To help you keep seeing the funny, and fun, side of life with your baby, arrange for a close family member or your partner to babysit and meet up with some uplifting friends for a drink or meal, or go to see a funny movie, for example. If you are staying in, why not watch a DVD or read a book that you know will make you laugh out loud.

Ha Ha

Ho Ho

Bottle-top *mobile*

Collect plastic milk or water bottle lids and wash them thoroughly. Pierce a hole in the center of each lid with a metal skewer and string them, like an abacus, onto a piece of twine. Secure each end of the twine in a tight knot. Tie each end of the twine to a table leg so it sits horizontally and is taut, and show your baby how to spin the lids and move them back and forth.

Twenty times
try-out

Your baby may take a while to eat a new food, since he needs to see, touch, and taste it first. Experts believe that babies may need to experience a new food up to 20 times before eating it. To make this activity playful and without pressure, make patterns on a plate with the food, or give it a personality—make mashed potato or cauliflower look like a sheep, for example. Keep putting the new food in his bowl and encourage him to touch and squeeze it; eventually it will get to his mouth.

Play in the grass

Babies love new and different sensations. Put your baby in some lush grass and let him feel the grass tickling his bare feet. Pick a blade of grass and gently stroke his arms, legs, and the soles of his feet with it. Pack a picnic lunch and a picnic blanket if you want to make the activity into more of an event.

MONTH 9

Clapping songs

If your baby is clapping now, sing lots of clapping songs such as "Patty-cake" and "If you're happy and you know it" for her to join in with you. Or sit your baby on the floor in front of you and try this action rhyme (you can also sing it to any tune). Why not have fun practicing together just before dinner time.

Clap, clap, clap your hands
Clap along with me,
Clap, clap, clap your hands
Until it's time for tea.

Additional verses:

Stamp, stamp, stamp your feet...
Pat, pat, pat your knees...
Touch, touch, touch your toes...

Gently hold her feet or hands in yours if she needs help to stamp her feet, pat her knees, or touch her toes. If she is enjoying herself, you may want to make up more verses, such as wiggling your hands, and let her watch and try to copy your actions.

9 MONTH

Mango popsicles

If your baby is ready for a new sensation, try a homemade popsicle so she can experience something very cold in her mouth. If she's teething, the icy fruit purée may also help soothe her gums. Mango is high in vitamin C and good for boosting the immune system, and is naturally sweet enough to not need the addition of sugar. Buy chunky wooden popsicle sticks and use very small non-PVC plastic containers as molds. Makes 6–8 popsicles.

ingredients
7 oz (200 g) fresh ripe mango cut into cubes
juice of half a lemon

method
1 Purée the cubes of fresh mango until smooth.

2 Mix the purée with the lemon juice and pour the mixture into 6–8 small egg molds. Press a wooden popsicle stick into the center of each and put in the freezer.

3 Once the popsicles are frozen, transfer them in their molds to a plastic container or freezer bag to prevent freezer burn.

4 To serve, remove a popsicle from the freezer and allow it to warm up a little; wait for a minute or so, or longer. To check if the popsicle is ready for your baby to eat, touch it with your clean finger to make sure it does not stick to your skin. Remove the popsicle from its mold, put a bib on your baby, since she may get a little messy, and hand her the popsicle to try.

Bench-press baby

Lie on your back on the floor with your knees bent and, supporting your baby carefully around her torso with your hands, raise her gently straight up in the air and down again. Make noises and silly expressions to encourage her to laugh. If she loves the sensation of being lifted up and down, turn this game into a set of bench presses, or push-ups, to tone your biceps as your baby has fun.

Take a trip to the playground

A busy playground with lots of other young children will fascinate your baby. She's old enough to sit in a baby bucket-shaped swing as you push her gently, or sit her on a baby slide, hold her around her waist if she can't sit without support, and walk alongside her as she slides down slowly. You can also put her in your lap as you move up and down on one end of a seesaw.

9 MONTH

Your baby may be ready for her first rocking toy. Try her on a baby rocker, holding her gently around the torso as it moves. If she enjoys it, borrow or buy a rocking toy, and sing "Rock-a-bye baby" as you rock her back and forth.

Rock-a-bye baby

Increase her vocabulary

Develop your baby's familiarity with different words by giving lots of emphasis to each word as you say it—for example, zip becomes "zzzippp"—and see if she can attempt to copy you.

Dressing with a point

As you dress your baby, point to each piece of clothing and identify it first so she becomes familiar with its name. She may even try to copy you and point to it herself. To make it more of a game, you could ask a question first, for example, "Where is your undershirt?," then point to it, hold it up, say "Here it is!" and dress her in it.

Baby squats

Your baby may be eager to pull up from sitting to standing now. Sit her in your lap, turn her around to face you, check that her feet are resting on your thighs, and support her torso as she practices using her leg muscles to stand up. Let her push up and squat back down as many times as she wants, giving her lots of praise and encouragement.

Rock 'n' roll

For this activity—an extension of tummy time (pp66–67)—put a cylindrical cushion, or bolster, or a large beach towel rolled up tightly, on a smooth floor and rest your baby, chest down, on the cushion. Hold her feet slightly off the ground and see if she attempts to push herself forward on her hands, or rock back and forth. Encourage her if need be by rolling her very gently along the floor.

Never-ending scarves

For a simple game of cause and effect, tie the ends of several colored silky scarves together. Pack them into an empty tissue box and then help your baby pull the length of scarves from the box. Talk about the texture and color of each as you do it, and let her feel them against her skin.

Reply
to your baby

At around nine months, your baby is likely to understand up to 20 familiar words that you regularly say to him, and he'll recognize your rhythm of speech. As a result, he may be including some new sounds, such as "t" and "w" when he's attempting to communicate with you. Pay attention to his babbling and reply by repeating his sounds and intonations back to him. He'll love this pretend conversation, and it will help him to become more confident in expressing himself.

This little piggy

Eight to nine months is a perfect age for your baby to enjoy the rhyme "This little piggy" and anticipate lots of tickles and laughter. Build the excitement by exaggerating your voice and actions as you count out each piggy on the toes of his foot and finish by tickling him all the way from the soles of his feet to his tummy:

This little piggy went to market,
This little piggy stayed at home,
This little piggy ate roast beef,
This little piggy had none,
And this little piggy cried
"Wee, wee, wee!" all the way home.

9
MONTHS

Indoor hide-and-seek

"Boo!"

For this easy version of hide-and-seek, arrange two chairs a short distance apart and put a heavy book on each chair seat to keep it stable and upright. Cover the chairs with a large sheet, or a tablecloth that reaches to the floor, to create a tent. Let your baby watch you put a stuffed animal inside the tent on the floor and then ask, "Where's teddy bear?" Help him lift the sheet to reveal the toy and say, "There's teddy bear!"

Your baby may have so much fun that he'll be happy to hide inside the tent to continue playing hide-and-seek. Get into the tent with him to begin with if necessary, and if he's relaxed about not being able to see you for a few seconds, let him "reappear" as you lift the sheet each time and express great surprise.

Maraca music

Now that your baby is spending more time exploring objects with her hands, her hand movements are becoming more controlled. Make a couple of homemade maracas for her to shake around and make some noise. Use mini food containers with tight lids and locking hinges and half-fill them with dried rice, macaroni, or beans. Make sure the lids are firmly snapped shut, seal them with tape, and show her how to shake the containers to make music.

Banana talk

Your baby's babbling is developing all the time. Pick up a banana and tell her that you are going to pretend it is a telephone and call someone she knows well. Have a brief conversation into the banana and pass it to your baby to babble into. Then peel the banana and enjoy eating it together.

"Cooking" with flour

Spread some newspaper or a plastic tablecloth on the floor, sit your baby on it—or in her high chair—and put a little pile of flour in front of her. Show her how to move the flour around with her hands and make squiggles, and give her a measuring spoon or small plastic cup to scoop up and play with the flour. Sprinkle some flour on her hands or feet so she can explore the sensation of it on her skin.

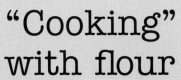

Make a sensations rug

Try changing from touch and feel books by making a sensations rug. Firmly sew some large swatches of textured materials—fur, soft velvet, and shiny, bumpy, rough, and reflective materials—onto a clean piece of fabric. Encourage your baby to sit on the rug and feel the different textures against her skin as you describe them to her.

Story time
with a twist

Make up short stories with your baby as the central character and include some of his favorite toys in each story.

Sam and Monkey's
jungle adventure

Sam woke up one morning and decided to go on an adventure. "Where shall we go today?" he asked Monkey. "Let's go to the jungle. Some of our favorite friends live in the jungle," said Monkey with a big smile.

Sam and Monkey set off for the jungle. They went through some long green grass to get there. But a big noise made them stop. It went "Rooooaarr!" Sam and Monkey stopped and hugged each other. "What was that?" The big noise came out of the long grass. It was only Lion, who wanted to say hello.

3

Sam and Monkey arrived at the jungle and looked up at the big trees. Then a long stick beside them moved. "Hide!" said Monkey. So Sam and Monkey hid until the long stick said "Hissssss." "Oh, it's only Snake," said Sam. "He's one of our favorite friends."

Sam and Monkey waved bye-bye to Snake. Then something in the jungle said "Squeak!" Monkey jumped into Sam's arms and Sam had to give Monkey a big hug. "Monkey, it's only a mouse. Let's go home for lunch." So Sam and Monkey went home and told everyone about meeting their favorite friends—and a mouse.

4

MONTH 9

187

Rearrange your kitchen cupboards

A low-level cupboard or drawer of baby-friendly kitchen equipment may keep your baby entertained for far longer than some of her toys. Even if you're tight on space, try to reorganize and store your plastic cups, plates, bowls, and Tupperware storage containers where they are easy for her to reach for and remove. Why not include a plastic spoon or scoop in a small cardboard box, or add some soft balls or pompoms to a plastic bowl for her to discover and play with.

Outdoor peekaboo

9 MONTH

At this age, your baby is just beginning to understand that you being out of sight doesn't mean that you aren't there anymore, and that eventually you will reappear. Play peekaboo when you are out for a walk in the park to reinforce the idea of person permanence. Hide your face behind your hat or an umbrella, or hide behind a park bench or a nearby tree so she can still see your body, and then pop your head out with a silly expression on your face as you say "peekaboo!"

In and *out* games

Putting objects into a box or basket and then dumping them out can become an appealing game for your curious baby. Give her a shoe box or a similar container, help her fill it with a few toys, soft balls, or empty yogurt containers, then let her dump them out onto the floor and start again.

You did it!

Cause-and-effect toys are really fun now. Let your baby press the doorbell of your house and listen to it ring, help her roll a toy down a sloping path, or show her how to press the buttons of a pop-up toy. Praise her by saying, "You did it!" and explain what she has done so she understands that her actions have caused a particular effect.

Your baby at...
9–10 months

As your baby is now more **mobile** and becoming an *explorer*, **playtime** is getting more *adventurous*. This is a **significant** month for him as he starts to **control** the *pincer movements* of his **fingers**, which may mean that he is learning how to *drop* and *throw* objects. He may also be practising how to *wave* bye-bye, and perhaps *point* to something he wants. He's making a greater effort to *communicate* with you, too, and may be **starting to say** "mama" and "dada".

by this age

your baby is probably able to:

🌸 Pick up, drop, and throw objects

🌸 Giggle and laugh

🌸 Use a pincer grip with his thumb and forefinger

🌸 Wave bye-bye

🌸 Respond to his name

🌸 Join in a "first conversation" with you as you both take turns to speak and listen to each other

Some babies may even be able to:

🌸 Start saying "mama" and "dada"

🌸 Point with their finger

Create a photo scrapbook

Fill a scrapbook with photos of your baby's favorite places and activities to create a travelog. This is a great tool for pointing to and talking about what you enjoy doing together, and when he is a toddler you will be able to use it as a prompt for him to choose where he would like to go.

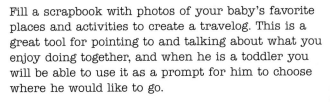

Body and soul

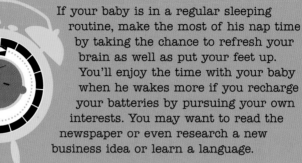

If your baby is in a regular sleeping routine, make the most of his nap time by taking the chance to refresh your brain as well as put your feet up. You'll enjoy the time with your baby when he wakes more if you recharge your batteries by pursuing your own interests. You may want to read the newspaper or even research a new business idea or learn a language.

Make a seesaw for a teddy bear

If your baby is having fun dropping and throwing his toys, try this game. Place a sturdy cardboard tube on the floor and rest a large, thin hardcover book or board on it to make a seesaw. Put a stuffed animal on one end of the book, press down sharply on the other end with your hand, and watch teddy fly up. Then go get the toy together. Your baby will love to watch his teddy bear travel through the air, and at the same time he'll be learning to track an object by following it with his eyes, and practice picking up his toy.

Budding gardener

Fill a child's watering can with a little water and help your baby hold onto the handle of the can. Keep your hand over hers to guide her and support the weight of the can as she tips water onto flowers in the garden. A raised flower bed is ideal, since she'll be able to hold onto the edge. If she's not yet standing, kneel down on the ground and let her sit on your lap to water the plants. She'll enjoy being your helper in this exciting new environment, and may even try to pull some weeds with you—all great practice for her manual dexterity.

Create a water garden

If you don't have any outside space, make a water garden. Pour a little water into a shallow plastic bowl or dish. Float a few flower heads on the water—nasturtiums, pansies, or rose petals are all good choices (check first before you use other flowers, since some can be poisonous). You could also add a few fronds of kale to the water to look like aquatic plants. Float some plastic ducks on top and let your baby have fun splashing around trying to catch the floating ducks with her hands.

If you want to extend the game, add a few drops of natural food coloring to the water and describe to your baby how you can see the color spread through the water. Then add another color and watch how the look of the water changes.

MONTH 10

Share a special snack

Introduce healthy foods that you will all enjoy. You could make guacamole and share it with your baby. Keep a close eye on your baby as she gums or eats these foods. Any grown-up treats, such as sour cream or spicy salsa, can be added on the side for adults. Set them well out of reach of your baby.

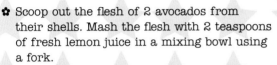

- ✿ Scoop out the flesh of 2 avocados from their shells. Mash the flesh with 2 teaspoons of fresh lemon juice in a mixing bowl using a fork.
- ✿ Chop 1 tomato and add it to the avocado mix.
- ✿ Stir gently, and transfer to a shallow bowl.
- ✿ Toast some bread or pitas and slice into strips. Serve with steamed carrots, strips of red pepper, and cucumbers cut lengthwise.

10 MONTH

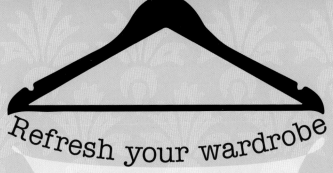

Refresh your wardrobe

If your body has changed a little since you had your baby, you may now have time to rethink your wardrobe. Treat it like a seasonal edit: rearrange your wardrobe so you can easily see the clothes you currently like to wear. If you have storage space, pack away clothes that don't seem to fit quite right at the moment. If you enjoy visiting secondhand stores, turn the event into a weekly outing with your baby to search for a pre-loved item. Or take a shopping trip to buy a new top or piece of jewelry if you need to pull an outfit together—whatever works for you.

Hidden music

Your baby is learning about object permanence—that an object he can't see may still be there. Wind up or start a musical toy, or even use a radio, and hide it under a blanket where it will be easy for your baby to hear it. Ask him where the sound is coming from and crawl around with him to find it, or ask him to point to where the sound is if he's not crawling yet. Praise your baby when he finds the toy. As you repeat the game and your baby understands what to look for, find other places—under pillows, or behind furniture—to hide the musical toy.

Ocean bottle

Fill a small plastic water bottle three-quarters full of water. Add a little blue food coloring to turn the water pale blue. Add some small shells and small brightly colored toy fish; if you don't have any on hand, make some simple fish shapes from tinfoil. Seal the top very tightly. Show your baby how to shake the bottle so the water forms bubbles and ripples and the fish swim. When the contents settle, he can study the shells and fish at the bottom of the bottle, then shake it again.

10 MONTH

Teddy bears' picnic

Whether it's a nice day and you can sit outside, or you make this a rainy day activity indoors, your baby will love to sit with you on a rug with lots of teddy bears and stuffed animals around you, and may happily talk and babble to herself. If you have a play tea set, give your baby and each animal a plate and cup and share some baby snacks. This is a great way to introduce your baby to imaginative play.

Try these...

Community matters

Visit your local town hall, library, or community center to pick up details of drop-in activities available to you and your baby. There may be activities—some free—such as mommy-and-me groups, dads' sessions, library story times, and swimming lessons.

Introduce a question

As you play or as your baby eats a snack, introduce questions such as "More?" or "All gone?" with a raised tone, a lift of the eyebrows, and your head tilted. These words will form part of his earliest vocabulary and will help him let you know what he wants.

Swap chores

If you're bored with always doing the vacuuming and your partner has had enough of doing the household administration, swap tasks for a week.

10 MONTH

Plan a treat

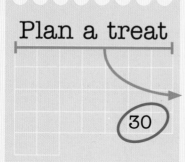

30

Your baby is at a good age to start being taken care of by a familiar grandparent or close relative overnight, so you may want to plan a night away while they babysit. If you can't find a babysitter, make plans for a special night in. If you are on your own, invite a friend or two over, order takeout, and plan some fun time together.

Young musician

Let your baby "play" a piano: help her use her fingers to press down on the piano keys. You can also use a keyboard or toy keyboard.

IN and OUT

Build your baby's understanding of position: play games that explore "in" and "out" by mailing a letter together, taking a toy out of the toy basket, and playing with a shape sorter. Repeat the words as you play.

Descriptive words

When you're out for a walk with your baby, add simple descriptive words—"tall tree," "little dog," and "fast bus"—as you name what you see to support his language development.

small

tall

Dropping objects

Your baby loves dropping things, but he's also very willing to help with chores that utilize his new skill. Pop him on your knee or sit together and give him some toys to drop into the toy box or rolled up socks to aim into an open drawer.

Make a noise!

Show your baby how to make a noise by holding the handles of two toy plastic mugs, one in each hand, and banging the cups together. This will help to improve his understanding of cause and effect.

Bonding
with family

Strengthen your baby's bond with her extended family: aunts, uncles, and cousins all make up her wider family network so why not arrange a family get-together for those who live within traveling distance. A picnic, barbecue, or potluck lunch can be a great way for your little one to get to know everybody. She no longer needs to be in your arms to feel safe, but stay nearby so she can keep you in sight when she's with others.

10 MONTH

Add sounds to feelings

By now your baby loves to communicate with you—and her listening skills are also improving. Introduce some new sounds that she will hear repeatedly and pick up to help her make herself understood in time. For example, if a toy tips over, say, "Uh oh, bear fell down," or try "Aahh, dolly is sleeping," and "Wheeeeee, baby is bouncing."

Create
a sensory
tunnel

Now that your baby is a young explorer, she is eager to explore the world around her. If she likes to play in toy tunnels, create your own sensory play tunnel. Turn a couple of large cardboard boxes on their sides, remove the tape from the bottoms to open up both ends, and connect them to make a tunnel that your baby can crawl through easily. Make a small hole in the roof and stuff a long sock through the hole so it dangles down into the tunnel. Tie a big knot in the top of the sock so it stays in position. Repeat with other brightly colored socks (check that they dangle down at different heights), and fill a few of the socks with scrunched-up newspaper and a baby's rattle. Encourage your baby to crawl through the tunnel with the socks brushing against her as she crawls. If she likes sitting inside it, cut a few peepholes in the sides so she can see you, add a few toys, and turn it into a fort, or let her lie inside and kick at the socks.

Knotted socks

Box

tunnel

Express emotions

Your baby is starting to learn about different emotions as she watches you and sees how you react to different situations. She will soon be copying you as she starts to show her emotions through her own behavior and body language, so introduce the concept by demonstrating some of your own emotions—happy, mad, surprised, sad—very simply and obviously as you talk to her.

Suitcase
sandbox

Find an old suitcase with rigid sides in the attic, or look for one in a secondhand store. Make sure that you can close and lock the lid between playtimes. Put a mat on the floor, and the suitcase on top, and pour some sand into the bottom of the case. Sit your baby in the sand and play by hiding her hands and feet in the sand; express surprise when she lifts them out. Then turn her palms face up and trickle sand through her fingers. You can also help her make patterns in the sand with her fingers.

Develop your baby's
taste buds

Take the opportunity to experiment with a greater range of flavors at mealtimes before your baby hits the stage when she wants to stick to the foods she knows she likes. Try switching between savory and sweet, and mild and sharp, foods to broaden her tastes: some grated cheese then mango, for example, or cottage cheese then banana bread, hard-boiled egg then apple, or sliced turkey then kiwi.

Sticky toys

Boost your baby's hand control by teaching her to grip and pull. Attach a strip of double-sided contact tape or strong sticking tape to a piece of cardboard or the side of a cupboard. Stick some soft toys onto the sticky strip and encourage your baby to try to pull them off (at this stage soft toys are safest and easiest for her to pull off).

Arrange a
musical playdate

Although your baby is still too young to play cooperatively with other children, he is starting to take more of an interest in the people around him. Invite your friends and their babies over for a music session: sit in a circle on the floor with your babies in your laps and sing some favorite action songs and rhymes together; the actions will help to develop the babies' gross motor skills. You should get a chance to share some laughter with your friends and your babies will enjoy watching each other and you.

You could also have a selection of rattles, maracas, and other simple toy instruments for the babies to play with.

10 MONTH

I'm a little teapot

I'm a little teapot.
Short and Stout.

Here is my handle,
(one hand on hip)
Here is my spout.
(other arm out straight)

When I get all steamed up,
Hear me shout

Just tip me over,
And pour me out!
*(lean over and tip arm
out like a spout)*

Row, row, row your boat

Row, row, row your boat
*(rock backward and forward pretending
to row a boat)*
Gently down the stream,
Merrily, merrily, merrily, merrily,
Life is but a dream.

Row, row, row your boat
Gently down the stream,
If you see a crocodile,
Don't forget to scream!

Row, row, row your boat
Gently down the river,
If you see a polar bear,
Don't forget to shiver.

Row, row, row your boat
Gently to the shore,
If you see a lion,
Don't forget to roar!

Baby pull-ups

Your baby will probably be developing the ability to stand upright from sitting while supported. Encourage her to start pulling herself up on her own by putting toys just out of reach on the sofa, on a chair, or on a bed, for example, so she wants to stand up by herself and stretch out her hand to grab them.

Shape-sorting
puzzles

Borrow or buy a couple of simple shape-sorting puzzles and help your baby find the correct holes to slot the different-shaped pieces into.

Moving objects

Your baby finds moving objects irresistible, which is all part of her developing an understanding of cause and effect. If she hasn't started already, she may soon be pushing toys such as cars and trains along the floor with her hands. She will also be fascinated by a bead maze; show her how the beads move along the wire so that she can practice her pincer grip by moving them herself.

Tube talk

Hold a cardboard tube near your baby's ear and gently whisper some words through it. She will turn her head to register where the sounds come from and to listen to what you are saying. Then give her the tube to babble into. She will start to understand the concept of taking turns if you take back the tube to talk to her again. Then for an added sensation, whisper against her skin so she feels your breath as you speak.

MONTH 10

Your baby at...
10-11 months

At this age your baby is learning to *play* with toys as they are intended to be used, such as **pushing** a car across the floor and **trying to slot** shapes into shape sorters—and he's growing more *self-confident* as he does so. He is working hard to *move around* more easily and **stand alone,** and to be *more involved* in the world around him using his growing **communication skills.**

by this age
your baby is probably able to:

- ❀ Stand upright with support
- ❀ Understand concepts such as "in" and "out"
- ❀ Cruise sideways for a few steps
- ❀ Point with his finger
- ❀ Let go of objects in his hand when he wants to
- ❀ Play with shape shorters, simple puzzles, and moving toys

Some babies may even be able to:
- ❀ Drink from a cup

Finger-paint art

Babies are fascinated by their ability to make marks, and your baby will love to explore how to create art using his hands. Playing with paint will also help him gain confidence in expressing himself with mark-making materials.

To make your own nontoxic, edible paint

✿ Mix together 4 tablespoons each of cornstarch and boiling water. The mixture will thicken quickly to a paste. Gradually whisk in enough boiling water to achieve a consistency similar to heavy cream. Divide between shallow bowls and add a few drops of natural liquid food coloring to each to make a bright color. Allow to cool.

✿ Put a large wipe-clean mat on the floor or on a table that you can sit at with your baby on your knee and tape a large sheet of paper to the mat.

✿ Put an old undershirt on your baby, or take his top off, put the bowls down together or one at a time, and let him make splashy art with his hands.

Develop your baby's creativity

✿ Show him how to make different marks on the paper. Or help him make thumb, finger, and handprints in different colors, then use a felt-tip pen to turn the prints into fish swimming in the water, birds, a garden of flowers, or insects such as ladybugs or crickets hopping across the page.

✿ Try dipping a wide strip of fabric into the paint and show your baby how to drag and swish it around the paper to make trailing marks.

✿ Make a mirror image of his marks by folding the piece of paper in half, then reveal it to him with a "Taa daa!" as you open up the two halves.

11 MONTH

Cruise control

If your baby has been crawling for a while, he may be wanting to spend more time on his feet and perhaps trying to walk, so help him learn how to cruise with confidence. Line up a couple of sturdy children's chairs and help him walk a few steps sideways as he holds on to each chair. Reassure him gently if he falls, and put a favorite toy on the farthest chair if he needs a little encouragement to walk.

Food faces

Keep mealtimes fun by serving your baby's food as a face before cutting it into bite-sized pieces—or help him make a face with the pieces. Try halved cherry tomatoes, coarsely grated cheese, cooked carrots, peas, and noodles, or a banana with halved strawberries and grapes and soaked raisins. Name the parts of the face as he eats them.

Exploring the night sky

Your baby's understanding and interest in the world around her is growing. Just before bedtime, look outside at the night sky with your baby and show her the moon and the stars or—especially in spring and summer, when it might still be light out when she goes to sleep—use a picture book with pictures of the moon and stars. Explain what they are and repeat this traditional lullaby:

Twinkle twinkle little star,
How I wonder what you are.
Up above the world so high,
Like a diamond in the sky.

Twinkle twinkle little star,
How I wonder what you are.

Or try this this one:

I see the moon,
And the moon sees me,
As it floats so high
Over Mummy and me.

I see the stars,
And the stars see me,
As they shine in the sky
Above Daddy and me.

Make a night sky mobile

A mobile of a moon, stars, and clouds floating above her crib will entrance your baby.

- ✿ Buy a mobile frame with predrilled holes (available online or at craft stores), or use a painted stick.
- ✿ Draw templates of a star, moon, and cloud on tracing paper. Pin the paper templates onto colored felt and cut out two shapes for each star, moon, and cloud. Alternatively, draw several stars, clouds, and a moon right onto stiff cardboard, cut them out, and paint them gold and silver.
- ✿ Sew each pair of felt shapes together using a blanket stitch, leaving a 1 in (2.5 cm) hole. Stuff each shape with toy filling; use the end of a pencil to work the filling into all the corners. Then sew up each hole.
- ✿ Attach the end of a long length of thread with a knot in the end onto the top of each felt or cardboard shape using a needle.
- ✿ Arrange the shapes around the mobile or along the length of the stick and tie the thread securely in place so the shapes hang down from the frame.
- ✿ Hang the mobile out of your baby's reach.

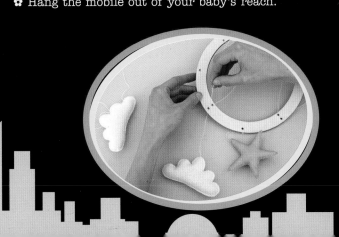

Even if you book a night or two away at a child-friendly hotel or campsite in the country or near the beach, you all going away together is an exciting family milestone.

If you are expecting even light sun, don't forget to pack sunscreen with a minimum SPF of 30 with UVA and UVB protection, and a sun hat for your baby. Pack some of your baby's favorite instant snacks (such as rice cakes) in resealable sandwich bags for the day. If you are going to the beach, why not take a lightweight pop-up child's tent to give your baby shade—especially at nap time—and a small beach ball, and a bucket and shovel to make sand castles together!

Little chef

As you prepare a meal, put your baby in his high chair so he can watch and copy you. If you make a salad, for example, give him some grated carrot and raisins soaked in water, or couscous and sliced red pepper, in his own plastic bowl with a little spoon for him to mix them together. If you cook a pasta sauce, put a couple of halved cherry tomatoes and grated cheese or cucumber pieces in the bowl for him to "cook" with. Tell him what you are doing and why; he should enjoy copying you and practicing his hand control.

Sorting and swapping

Put your baby in your lap at a table, or pop him in his high chair, and set two empty bowls or plastic containers in front of him. Add a few whole lemons and mandarin oranges to one bowl and show him how to move them to the other bowl. This simple game allows you to talk about the concepts of shape and color, and full and empty, and he will enjoy moving the objects from one bowl to another.

Copycat
doing dishes

Now that your baby is more interested in the world around him and likes to join in, let him try washing dishes. Spread a plastic mat over the floor if necessary. Place a large plastic bowl containing a little soapy water on the floor, add a couple of bright cups, a few plastic spoons, and a bath toy or two, and show him how you wash dishes. Then let him try to copy you, and have fun splashing the water with his hands.

MONTH 11

Sleepy stretches

Sit with your baby facing you so she can watch you and try to copy what you do as you say this rhyme and do the actions. Then repeat the words, helping your baby to try some of the stretches:

- ✿ Stretch up high, as high as a tree
  (stretch your arms up above your head).
- ✿ Curl up as small as a buzzy bumble bee
  (curl up, with your arms wrapped around your knees).
- ✿ Now we're feeling very sleepy
  (make a big yawn).
- ✿ Relax your hands, relax your feet
  (let your hands and your feet go limp).
- ✿ Close your eyes and let's go fast to sleep
  (put your hands together and rest them against the side of your head).

11 MONTH

Laundry in the fast lane

Rather than use your baby's precious nap time to get the laundry done, why not do it together? Although the work may take you longer, it will be more fun for you both and can help free up nap times for you to have some time for yourself.

✿ Position your laundry basket on the floor next to your baby. Sit her down inside the basket, lightly cover her with a clean dish towel, and pretend you can't find her; she'll giggle when you say, "Oh no, where is my baby?" Make her laugh again as you remove the dish towel and "discover" her.

✿ Then turn the laundry basket into a car and make the relevant noises as you gently zoom her around the room. Stop between each round of the racetrack to hang up or fold some laundry or unload the washing machine. Repeat the words "Pit stop!" each time you stop, and describe what you are doing; she'll soon anticipate this stop/start routine as part of the game.

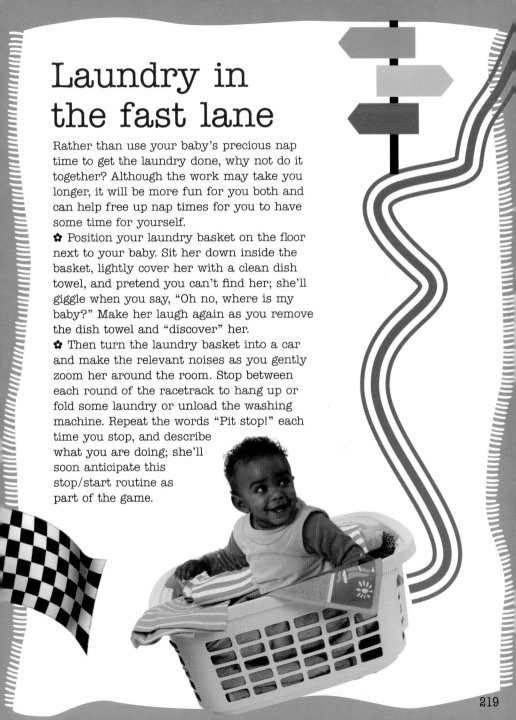

Try these...

Beat to the rhythm

Tap out a single beat on an upturned saucepan either with your hand or a plastic or wooden spoon and see if your baby can copy you. Build up to making two or three beats.

Helping out

Your baby may be ready to act out familiar routines himself. Let him "change" his teddy by popping a disposable diaper onto the teddy so he can pull it off. Let him help you put toys back in the toy box, or give him a damp cloth to play by wiping a table.

Stacking rings

Help develop your baby's hand–eye coordination by taking turns to slide a few large plastic toy rings, or baby-friendly rings of twisted rope, onto your arm—or put smaller curtain rings onto the handle of a wooden spoon.

Start a babysitting circle

Have child care you can trust without the expense by inviting some good friends to make up a group. Find a babysitting circle website online that makes it easy to send group emails and give each other babysitting "credits" to use.

Stuck together

Sit back-to-back on the floor with your partner or a friend and encourage your baby to squeeze in between you to separate you both. When you have made room for him in between you, pretend to gently squish him to make him laugh and giggle.

It's a goal!

Turn a large cardboard box into a goal and encourage your baby to roll some soft balls into it. Shout, "It's a goal!" when a ball goes in.

Unwrap

At bath time, wrap a small bath toy in a wash cloth. Give it to your baby to unwrap and ask him what he has discovered, then tell him what it is. Repeat with other favorite bath toys.

Out and about

Naming things can make any outing fun. Use the "real" name for what you see then make the noise: "It's a truck and it goes 'Vroom, vroom,'" or "Here's a dog, it says 'Woof, woof.'".

Hide-and-seek

For this advanced version of peekaboo, ask an older child or friend who will happily join in to hide in the room. Ask your baby where they are. Help him find them and call out "Peekaboo!" as they pop out. Or hide a teddy bear and play peekaboo in the same way.

Peekaboo!

Roly-poly
pictures

Find a large cylindrical container or tube and paste some brightly colored photos or pictures from magazines on the outside. Use images that are familiar to your baby, such as favorite animals, toys, and people. Cover the cylinder in a clear self-adhesive wrap. Help your baby roll it along the floor. When it comes to rest, point to a picture you can see, talk about it, and make all the appropriate noises.

Let's go fly a kite

Your baby is eager for new adventures outside. Expand her horizons and stimulate her senses by watching kites flying in the sky at the park or the beach on a windy day—or fly your own kite. Use a small children's kite and let her help you hold onto the kite strings from the safety of her stroller: make sure the kite strings are secure in your hands and then place your hands over hers (don't attach the string to her hand or to the stroller). She'll love to watch the brightly colored kite dancing in the sky.

11 MONTH

Bouncing monkey

Stand your baby in the middle of a bed, hold her firmly by the waist, and let her bounce up and down as you say or sing the rhyme, "Five little monkeys bouncing on the bed":

Five little monkeys bouncing on the bed,
One fell off and bumped his head.
Mommy called the doctor and the doctor said,

"No more monkey business bouncing on the bed!"

Four little monkeys... **Three** little monkeys...

Two little monkeys... **One** little monkey...

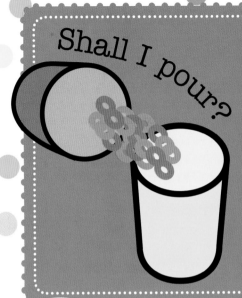

Shall I pour?

Sit on the floor on a blanket or cotton sheet with your baby. Put some dry, o-shaped cereal in two plastic, paper, or stacking cups. Show your baby how to pour the cereal from one cup to another and let him try to pour the cereal himself. It will take him many tries to get his hand coordination right, but he will love to spend time doing this activity and enjoy eating some of the cereal too.

Learning about feelings

The more animated you are when you talk about feelings with your baby, the more comfortable he will be expressing himself. Give his soft toy animal a hug to demonstrate how to show love, show the emotion on your face, and describe what you are doing and feeling. Then give him his toy to hug. Or, for example, say that the toy is happy to be reading with Daddy as you give your baby a big smile.

You can also use soft toys to act out the emotional content in story books: when a character reacts with feeling, stop reading and act out the emotion with a toy, showing the expression on your own face and emphasizing your body language as you talk.

11 MONTH

Boom!

Sit on the floor on either side of an empty plastic bowl and take turns dropping an easy-to-grip bean bag or ball into the bowl. Say "Boom!" as the bean bag hits the base of the bowl to make your baby giggle. Sprinkle some flour into the bowl if you want flour dust to fly up as the bean bag hits the base to give him a greater sense of cause and effect.

Shoot and splash

Your baby is grasping concepts such as "in" and "out" now. Develop his understanding of this by resting a long tube, large enough to hold a bouncy ball, over the edge of a saucepan or bowl filled with water. Show your baby how to put the ball into one end of the tube so it rolls out at the other end into the water. Describe how quickly or slowly the ball moves through the tube and reappears as you tip the tube up and down—he'll be intrigued by what is happening.

Floor art

If you don't have space to cover your floor in paper (see right), cut the shape of a baby from a large piece of cardboar put it on the floor, and guide yo baby's hand to make marks for mouth, nose, eyes, and hair. Cut clothes from more card and let h scribble on them. She may want help you pat down the clothes if you stick them in place with a dal of nontoxic, child-friendly glue. Talk about the person you are making as you play.

Letting your baby scribble and make marks on paper is fun for her and improves her fine motor skills by strengthening the smaller muscles in her fingers. It also helps improve her hand—eye coordination. Buy some very chunky, nontoxic, child-friendly crayons and a cheap roll of plain paper—or recycle a leftover roll of wallpaper and use the plain side. Cover a large area of the floor with the paper and tape the paper down at the edges.

✿ Sit on the floor with your baby and guide her hand (if she wants your help) to make different marks on the paper.

✿ Lie her down on the paper, draw an outline around her, and let her scribble inside to fill in the silhouette.

✿ Draw simple shapes and patterns and name them all for her.

✿ At the end of your drawing session, cut out some of her art and stick it into a scrapbook.

Texture track

If your baby loves cars and toys with wheels, create a mini course of different textures for him to explore and understand how quickly or slowly his toy moves.

Lay a large mat on the floor. Fold a piece of stiff cardboard in half and cover one half in tinfoil to make a smooth, slippery surface. Position the folded card on the mat to make a ramp and arrange a tray with a thin layer of fine sand at the base of the smooth, slippery slope.

Talk about different textures and speeds as you show your baby how to push the car up the cardboard slope, release the car in his hand so it rolls down the smooth, shiny ramp, and comes to a halt in the grainy sand. See if your baby can learn to wait for the action word "Go!" before releasing the car to roll down the ramp.

Memory game

Place two colored blocks that are different shapes and sizes (make sure they look very different) in front of your baby. Describe one block as you pick it up: "This is the big yellow block." Then put it behind your back. Ask your baby where the block is. He may point and make sounds to show you he knows where it is. Repeat with the other block.

Color hunt

Tape four different colored squares (or paint them) onto a large piece of cardboard. Set the cardboard on the floor and walk around the house with your baby looking for different objects to match each colored square—a lemon for a yellow square and a blue sponge for a blue square, for example. Talk to your baby about what colors you are looking for as you search. Pile the objects on top of the matching color and name the color again as you do so. He can easily recognize different colors by now, although he won't be naming them himself for another two years or so.

MONTH 11

Your baby at...

11–12 months

As your baby approaches his **first birthday,** you will be amazed at how far he has progressed. He is a *unique personality* bursting with **energy** and **curiosity.** He's also able to *express a wide range of emotions*, and his **attention span** is **growing.** He's getting ready to *talk,* can do more for himself *physically*, expresses his *emotions* more easily, and enjoys lots of **stimulation** and **excitement!**

by this age
your baby is probably able to:

* Say his first words

* Imitate some words

* Take his first steps

* Find hidden objects easily

* Use gestures such as shaking his head for "no"

* Play "jokes"

* Stack blocks

Some babies may even be able to:

* May be able to scribble using chunky crayons and chalk

* Enjoy imaginative play

Make a story time fort

Story time is probably a big feature of your baby's bedtime routine by now, but reading stories in the day is also a great way to wind down after a busy morning, or make the transition from an exciting activity to a quiet time. Why not make a story time fort by arranging a soft blanket and lots of cushions or pillows on the floor under the dining room table, or behind the sofa. Hang a couple of large sheets or blankets over the sides of the table, or over the back of the sofa, to create a tent shape, and anchor down the edges of the sheets with books or shoes. Snuggle up together on the cushions and use a flashlight to spotlight the pictures as you read stories to her.

12 MONTH

Birthday celebration

It's nearly your baby's first birthday, so celebrate her journey by planning a party with all your relatives and friends, or with just a few special people depending on her personality and how social she is.

Don't forget it's your anniversary as parents too, and a cause for celebration. You may want to get a babysitter and go out another evening, or celebrate at home.

1st

Hidden treasure

At the beach or in a sandbox, show your baby a brightly colored object and cover it with sand while she watches you. Ask her to find the object by helping her dig into the sand. Gradually you can start hiding the treasure when she's not looking; she will quickly build on her understanding of object permanence and how things disappear and reappear.

First birthday
silhouette

A framed silhouette of your baby at 12 months makes a wonderful memento to mark his first birthday. Make several if you want to have one as a keepsake for yourself and give some away to family members. Take a photo of your baby for the silhouette, making sure he holds his head up so you can capture a clear profile of him.

1 Cut some patterned paper to fit a frame using a craft knife, ruler, and cutting mat. This will make up the background.

2 Using tracing paper, trace around a photo of your baby's profile, then cut out the template with a pair of scissors.

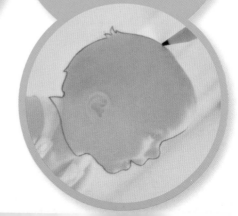

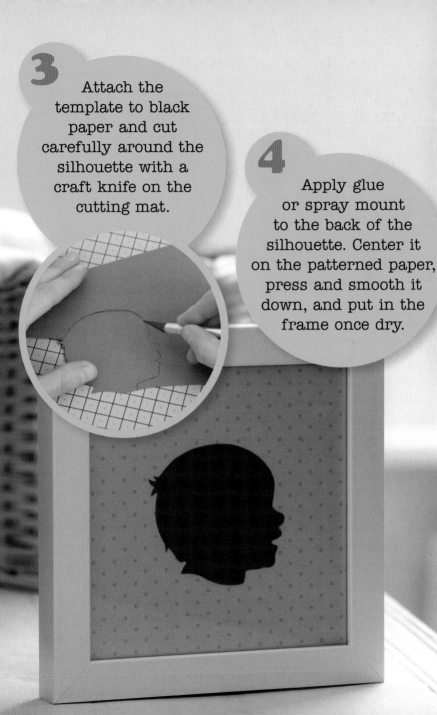

3 Attach the template to black paper and cut carefully around the silhouette with a craft knife on the cutting mat.

4 Apply glue or spray mount to the back of the silhouette. Center it on the patterned paper, press and smooth it down, and put in the frame once dry.

235

Silly hats

Your baby is old enough to understand that you exist even if she
can't see you or hear your voice, so she should be relaxed about
you dressing up and pretending to be someone—or something—
else. Put various household objects, such as a colander, cardboard
box, open book, plastic bucket, and pair of shorts, on your head
and make her laugh by making funny faces and asking in a silly
voice if the hat looks good on you. Let her try on the safer objects.

Personalize your baby's space

You probably made your baby's sleeping area as soothing and as neutral as possible when she was a newborn, but now is a good time to adapt it to her personality. You can do something simple such as put a cork bulletin board on a wall to hold a couple of bright images, stand a large cardboard cutout of her favorite character in the corner, paint a simple stencil on the walls, or plan a larger project and redecorate the room. Be aware of the fact that her area must retain a peaceful enough atmosphere to encourage her to sleep.

Set up a book **corner**

Your baby is learning how to turn the pages of a book, and enjoy looking at the pictures herself, especially if there are also flaps, sounds, and textures to play with. Make a special area in your living space at home with some soft cushions or a rug on the floor for her book corner, and place a few of her favorite books in a decorated cardboard box or a basket for her to explore.

Bear hugs

Your baby is ready for you to **hold him against your chest** in a **hearty bear hug** and then **tickle him** to make him laugh.

Make your own

If your baby adores soft play and it's expensive to make frequent trips to a play center, create your own soft play area. Line an empty kiddie pool with an old comforter or a blanket. Arrange some sofa cushions on the floor around it. Fill the pool with brightly colored plastic balls that are very light to handle, or use sheets of newspaper scrunched up into balls. Seat your baby down in the paddling pool and show him how to swish his arms and move them like windmills to move the balls around.

soft play area

Chalk
drawings

Use some fat sticks of chalk to make patterns on a paved outdoor surface; your baby should be able to grab the chalk easily and make marks and scribbles with your guidance.

Hand
over
hand

Hold your hand out, palm down, and place your baby's hand on top of your outstretched hand. Lay your other hand on top of his, then ask him to put his other hand on top of yours. Pull your hand out from the bottom of the pile and place it onto the top. Repeat until your baby stops giggling.

MONTH 12

Try these...

Shaping sounds

Your baby's speech is moving along rapidly: she may be pointing and trying to name objects, so give her a chance to shape a sound or babble before you name the object for her.

Little helper

Give your baby a simple request, for example, "Please give me the cup." Point at what you want, nod encouragement, and she'll want to help by passing it to you.

Have a chat

She may love to babble, which has the rhythm and tone of a real conversation. Listen to her attentively when she's trying out sounds such as "ka" for "cup." Sit face to face, make eye contact, watch her lips so you can practice with her, and use the same rhythm as you repeat her words back to her. Enjoy this time "chatting" together—the process of gaining speech is one of incredible speed and complexity, so revel in how far she's come.

ka

Take a sled ride

Sit your baby down on a simple plastic sled, or a tin tray or plastic tray, and drag her smoothly across a gentle sand dune, a slightly sloping grassy lawn, or at the park if it has snowed. Show her how to draw shapes in the sand with your fingers or a stick if you are at the beach or in the snow.

Socialize online

Skype or FaceTime a relative or friend regularly while your baby sits on your knee so that other people can begin to bond with her and you can enjoy some support and friendship.

Sensory play

For a calming, sensory playtime activity, stir a few drops of lavender essential oil into a large bowl of dried rice, add a couple of cups and let your baby practice emptying and filling the cups with rice.

Think outside the gender toy box

Your baby is beginning to learn about imaginative play, so now is a good time to refresh the toy box. If you've got a boy you may have been given lots of trains and cars for him to play with, and if you've got a girl, dolls and tea sets maybe. Why not do a toy swap for a while with a friend who has a child of the opposite sex?

Playdough

Make a batch of homemade playdough and help your baby squeeze, press, and form the dough into all sorts of shapes. If you make some animals, describe what you are doing, and make the noise of the animal. Make a couple more batches in other bright colors if this becomes a favorite activity.

For 1 batch of colored playdough
- ✿ 3 cups flour
- ✿ 2 tbsp cornstarch
- ✿ 1 cup salt
- ✿ 1 cup cold water with 2 tsp liquid natural food coloring added
- ✿ 2 tsp vegetable oil

Put all the ingredients in a large bowl and combine with a spoon. When it forms a dough, put it onto a board and knead it with your hands until it takes on the look and consistency of playdough. Store in an airtight bag for up to 1 week.

Memory game

hide ball

Use three upside down plastic cups and a small ball. Show your baby the ball, then hide it under a cup as he watches you. Encourage him to point to or hit the cup with the hidden ball and praise him if he picks the right one—he's building his understanding of object permanence. As you repeat the game and he becomes practiced at finding the ball, try hiding it under a different cup.

12 MONTH

Board of
curiosities

If you—or a relative or friend—have some old household fixtures, make a play board of the safe objects. Use a sanded piece of MDF with no sharp corners. Recycle an old door handle, door bell, and security door chain and attach them firmly to the board so they are securely in place and your baby can safely turn the handle, press the bell and try to say "Ding-dong," and put the chain in the holder. If you have an old hinge, screw one half of the hinge to a piece of thin sanded wood with a door knob stuck on and attach the other half of the hinge to the board to make a flap for him to lift. He will enjoy thinking about how to push, pull, and lift these different objects. Watch him as he plays to make sure he doesn't chew or suck the board.

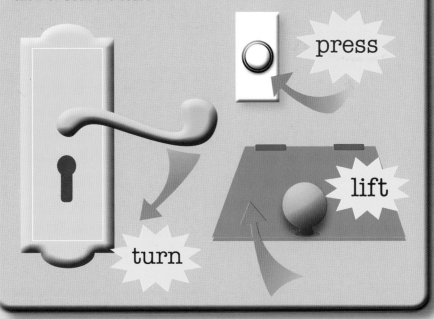

press

lift

turn

Bubbles on the breeze

POP!

Blow bubbles together outdoors on a bright day. Watch them as they float away on the breeze or drift to the ground, and try to pop them as they fall. If your baby is not walking yet, support her at the waist to stand and swipe at them.

Wooden puzzles

Puzzles are fantastic both as tabletop activities and problem-solving toys. Find some chunky puzzles for your baby that reveal a picture beneath each puzzle piece. Name the picture as she holds the knob and lifts the wooden piece up.

Make a mailbox

Cut a large rectangle in the lid of an old shoebox to make a mailbox shape. Give your baby some recycled envelopes or an old pack of cards and show her how to mail her "letters" through the hole. She will love to watch her letters disappear, and be revealed again as you open up the box. You could then go for an outing together to your local mailbox at collection time and watch the mail carrier bag up the mail.

Counting *rhymes*

Twelve months is an ideal age to start introducing rhymes and songs with a specific counting emphasis to your baby. Although it will be a while before she joins in, she will love the repetition and sense of anticipation as you count on your fingers and sing the words:

One, two, three, four, five,
Once I caught a fish alive,
Six, seven, eight, nine, ten,
Then I let it go again.

Why did you let it go?
Because it bit my finger so.
Which finger did it bite?
This little finger on the right.

MONTH 12

Toppling tower

Gather some empty cereal boxes, plastic bowls, empty yogurt containers, juice cartons, and light baby blocks. Help your baby build a tower with them—he's learning about shapes, sizes, and solidity, and how to put things together using his problem-solving ability, balance, and manual skills. Then knock the tower down together!

Help your baby build a tower

Make binoculars

Make a pair of binoculars with two cardboard tubes by taping them together. Look through them and describe one thing you can see, then let your baby look through the binoculars as you point to the object. Repeat the game with other objects and even family members.

Head,
shoulders,
knees and toes

Slowly sing or say this rhyme and place your hands on the parts of your body as you mention them. Help your baby to do the same. Then repeat the rhyme a little more quickly to make you both laugh:

Head, shoulders,
knees and toes,
knees and toes.

Head, shoulders,
knees and toes,
knees and toes.

Eyes and ears and mouth and nose.

Head, shoulders,
knees and toes,
knees and toes!

learn
to bl●w

Puff your cheeks out and blow gently on your baby's cheek, avoiding her eyes. She should enjoy the sensation. See if she can copy you by making a raspberry noise or taking a big breath out. Show her how you can blow a feather off the palm of your hand, or make a toy windmill's blades spin around, and let her try. Then read the story "The three little pigs" and demonstrate how to blow as you read. She may try to join in with you.

Colored foods

Arrange bite-sized pieces of different colored foods—such as red cherry tomatoes, blue blueberries, green avocado or cucumber, and yellow mango or banana—on a plate (bright and primary colors are easier for her to distinguish at this age than more subtle hues). Name the colors, then encourage her to eat up the pieces of food.

Feely bags

Use a cotton shoe or book bag as a feely bag and put some tactile objects inside it—perhaps a soft, furry toy, a hand-massage ball with rounded knobbles, a rattle, a wooden building block, and a scrunched up ball of newspaper. Show your baby how to put her hand inside the bag and feel for an object (you may have to help her find just one object to touch). She has the extra surprise of pulling the object out of the bag to discover what it is.

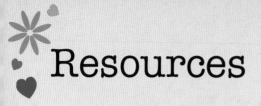

Resources

CHILD CARE

BabyCenter
www.babycenter.com
Offering general information, such as
how to read to your toddler.

Child Care Aware
www.childcareaware.org
Tel: 800-424-2246
Information and support for
working parents.

Children's Research Center
http://ecap.crc.illinois.edu/
Tel: 877-275-3227
Information for parents and families
on development, education, and care
of children.

Head Start
www.nhsa.org
Provides comprehensive child
development services to economically
disadvantaged children and families.

National Child Care Information Center
www.nccic.acf.hhs.gov
A clearinghouse linking parents to online
child-care related topics.

The National Organization of Mothers of Twins Clubs
www.nomotc.org
Tel: 248-231-4480
Support and information for families
of twins, triplets, and more.

Parenting Coalition International
www.parentingcoalition.org
Tel: 202-898-0808

Zero to Three
www.zerotothree.org/site/PageServer
Tel: 202-638-1144
Resources related to child care from
birth to three.

BREAST-FEEDING

La Leche League International
www.lalecheleague.org
Tel: 800-LALECHE
A service that offers breast-feeding advice
and information.

Women's Health
www.womenshealth.gov/breastfeeding
Tel: 800-994-9662
Tel: 888-220-5446 (TDD)
Government website with information on
breast-feeding.

MOTHER AND CHILD HEALTH

American Academy of Pediatrics
www.aap.org
Tel: 847-228-5005

American Association for Premature Infants
www.aapi-online.org
Tel: 513-956-4331
National organization providing support, information, and education for parents of premature babies.

American Red Cross
www.redcross.org
Tel: 800-REDCROSS
First aid and Safety.

Postpartum Depression (WebMd)
www.webmd.com/depression/
postpartum-depression/
Support and Information for women with postpartum depression.

Federation for Children with Special Needs
www.fcsn.org
Tel: 800-331-0688
A center for parents and parent organizations to work together on behalf of children with special needs and their families.

Healthy Mothers, Healthy Babies Coalition
www.hmhb.org
Tel: 703-837-4792
Information on the health and safety of mothers, babies, and families.

Safe Kids
www.safekids.org
Tel: 202-662-0600
Information on preventing childhood injury.

SUPPORT

American Academy of Child & Adolescent Psychology
www.aacap.org
Tel: 202-966-7300
Provides a national list of accredited child psychologists.

Step Family Association of America
www.stepfam.org
Information and support for step families.

HelpGuide.org
Parent Helpline: 1-888-435-7553
Crying Baby Hotline: 1-866-243-2229

Parents without Partners
www.parentswithoutpartners.org
Tel: 800-637-7974
Information and support for single parents.

Index

Acknowledgments

Claire Halsey would like to thank:

My parents, George and Patricia Higginbotham, for all the happy playtimes in my own childhood. Thanks also to my family, Michael, Rupert, Toby and Dominic, to Vicki McIvor for all her work on my behalf, and to Susannah Steel and all at DK who were, as ever, a joy to work with.

Dr. Claire Halsey is a mom of three and a consultant clinical psychologist of almost 30 years' standing, specializing in work with children and families. She is author of DK's *Baby Development - everything you need to know*, and co-author of DK's *Ask a Parenting Expert*.

Susannah Steel would like to thank:

Carolyn, Jeanette, and Annabel and their families for their suggestions, Claire Halsey for her excellent guidance and great conversations, and also James, Rosie, and Jessie.

Susannah Steel is a writer and editor, and a mother. Her work includes books on parenting, nutrition, fitness, women's health, and organic and eco-friendly lifestyles.

DK would like to thank:

Michèle Clark for the index, Claire Wedderburn-Maxwell and Katie Bone for proofreading, Mandy Earey and Tessa Bindloss for design assistance, and Martha Burley and Alice Kewellhampton for editorial assistance. The recipes on pages 135, 147, 163, 179, and 196 were taken from *Feeding your baby day by day* by Fiona Wilcock, a comprehensive guide to weaning, with over 200 recipes.